Engels Revisited

Engels Revisited

New Feminist Essays

Edited by Janet Sayers, Mary Evans, and Nanneke Redclift

Tavistock Publications
London and New York

First published in 1987 by
Tavistock Publications Ltd
11 New Fetter Lane, London EC4P 4EE

Published in the USA by
Tavistock Publications
in association with Methuen, Inc.
29 West 35th Street, New York, NY 10001

© 1987 Janet Sayers, Mary Evans, Nanneke Redclift

Typeset by MC Typeset Limited, Chatham, Kent
Printed in Great Britain
at the University Press, Cambridge

British Library Cataloguing in Publication Data

Engels revisited: new feminist essays.
  1. Engels, Friedrich
  I. Sayers, Janet II. Evans, Mary, *1946–*
  III. Redclift, Nanneke
  335.4'092'4   HX273.E56
  ISBN 0-422-60810-6

Library of Congress Cataloging in Publication Data

Engels revisited.
  (Social science paperbacks; 347)
  Bibliography: p.
  Includes index.
  1. Women and socialism. 2. Engels, Friedrich, 1820–1895
  — Views on women. I. Sayers, Janet. II. Evans, Mary,
  1936–   . III. Redclift, Nanneke. IV. Series.
  HX546.E55 1987   335'.0088042   86–14345
  ISBN 0-422-60810-6 (pbk.)

Contents

List of contributors

Janet Sayers is Lecturer in Psychology, University of Kent at Canterbury.

Mary Evans is Lecturer in Sociology, University of Kent at Canterbury.

Nanneke Redclift is Lecturer in Anthropology, University College, London.

Jane Humphries is Lecturer in Economics and Politics, and Fellow of Newnham College, Cambridge University.

Martha Gimenez is Professor of Sociology, University of Colorado at Boulder.

Moira Maconachie is currently living in South Africa.

Delia Davin is Lecturer in Social and Economic History, University of York.

Engels Revisited

1

Introduction: Engels, socialism, and feminism

Janet Sayers, Mary Evans, and Nanneke Redclift

The purpose of this volume is to commemorate the centenary of the publication in 1884 of Engels' *The Origin of the Family, Private Property and the State*. Written in three months, partly in response to August Bebel's *Woman in the Past, Present and Future*, *The Origin* was immediately popular and influential, in that it was rapidly integrated into the socialist agenda and became a major socialist text on the 'woman question'. Its recent rediscovery by feminists arises however from more than its centrality within socialism: Engels is important to contemporary feminists because he offers the possibility of a materialistic explanation for women's subordination and attempts to establish a relationship between the ownership of private property and the ideological subordination of women.

Yet although *The Origin* has always been regarded as an important contribution to Marxist theory (and one of the clearer expositions of Marx's theory of historical development) there have always been those who have expressed reservations about the implications and the analysis of the book. Leaders of the turn–of–the-century German SPD, men like Kautsky and Cunow, were critical of it from its very first appearance, rejecting as 'too redolent of bourgeois psychology the high value Engels reluctantly placed

on monogamy', and as misguided in holding that: 'the driving
force behind the transition from polygamy was women's longing
for "chastity", "temporary or lasting marriage with a single man",
or "deliverance"' (Porter 1980:67–8). In England, even those few in
socialist circles who were committed to Marxism – those involved
in the Marxist Social Democratic Federation of the beginning of the
century – objected to *The Origin*. The Federation's leader,
Hyndman, dismissed it as 'a colossal piece of impudence . . . to
garble Morgan's grand work' (Rowbotham 1973:72). Women of
the Socialist Party of America, influenced by Engels' *The Origin*,
were criticized by their leaders as bourgeois feminist in their
inspiration. At the same time in Russia socialists took issue with
The Origin as mistakenly treating the family as relatively autonomous from society and thereby returning Marxism to the dualism
and utopianism of *The German Ideology* (Vogel 1983:91). And this
view persisted in the USSR into the 1930s where *The Origin*'s
'belief in individual sex love and the rights of sexual life to be
beyond the province of the state' was characterized as 'bourgeois'
and 'irresponsible' (Millett 1971:175).

On the other hand, *The Origin* has also regularly been promoted
by socialist leaders. Lenin, for instance, recommended it as one of
the best means of answering the question: 'What is the state, how
did it arise and what fundamentally should be the attitude to the
state of the party of the working class, which is fighting for the
complete overthrow of capitalism – the Communist Party?' (Lenin
1919:3). Thirty years later, Harry Pollitt, then general secretary of
the British Communist Party, similarly recommended *The Origin*
which, he said, would 'help every one of us to win new allies in the
fight for peace, national independence and the advance of socialism'
(Pollitt 1950:6).

To socialist women the book has, inevitably, always been of
fundamental importance since it is virtually the only account within
Marxism of relations between the sexes and of the possible means
of uniting the struggle for social advance with sexual emancipation.
In the years immediately after its publication *The Origin* was
praised by Eleanor Marx, Clara Zetkin, Rosa Luxemburg, and
Ottilie Baader and inspired Zetkin, Luxemburg, and Baader in

their work in the women's section of the German SPD (see e.g. Thönnessen 1973; Draper and Lipow 1976; Porter 1980). What was stressed particularly by these women was Engels' assertion that the emancipation of women depends on their full integration into social production. Rosa Luxemburg, for instance, wrote elegaically of the liberating possibilities for women in work, even in the case of 'the music-hall dancer whose legs sweep profit into her employer's pocket' (Luxemburg 1971:220). She also went on to cite in support of her programme for women's emancipation not only Engels' scientific socialism but also Fourier's earlier utopian socialism. Today women in the Communist Party of the People's Republic of China likewise quote Engels in support of their belief that the emancipation of women depends on their large-scale entry into social production (Lu *et al.* 1972).

But while feminists and socialist women have found common cause in the belief that women should be liberated from economic dependence on men, there have always been differences of opinion about the nature and the extent of the social changes necessary to bring about this transformation. Bourgeois feminists campaign for women's right to paid work (and equal pay at work) and in so doing form common cause with socialist feminism and with Engels. Like socialist women, they too stress the emancipatory effect of material independence for women. More problematic – and consistently divisive – is the attitude which bourgeois feminists and socialist feminists take to the question of the links between patriarchy and capitalism and the importance of locating class conflict as a major cause of women's subordination in this debate. Engels still occupies a central role in this controversy, and feminists writing in the hundred years after the publication of *The Origin* have frequently returned to the book in an attempt to find further validation for their arguments. For example, in *The Second Sex* de Beauvoir maintained her position – of individualistic feminism and existentialist values – by opposition to what she described as Engels' excessive economic determinism (le Doeuff 1980:281). The same critique of Engels as a 'mere' materialist is to be found in Kate Millett's *Sexual Politics*, where she argues that: 'Engels supplied nothing but a history and economy of the patriarchal family, neglecting to investigate the mental habits it inculcates' (Millett 1971:169).

This humanist position suffered something of a reverse in the 1970s when, as Veronica Beechey pointed out at the conference on which this book is based, the 'scientific' (post 1867) socialism of Marx – and Engels – enjoyed a revival in popularity. The new materialism of Althusser *et al* attempted to eschew the vulgar Marxism of economism and the politics associated with this position by arguing that the 'determination in the last instance by the economy is exercised, according to the phases of the process, not accidentally, not for external or contingent reasons, but essentially, for internal and necessary reasons, by permutations, displacements and condensations' (Althusser 1970:213); or, as Engels put it in 1890: 'The economic situation is the basis, but the various elements of the superstructure . . . also exercise their influence upon the course of the historical struggles and in many cases preponderate in determining their form' (Engels 1890:682).

Thus in rediscovering materialism, contemporary feminists also inherited the theoretical problems central to materialism and Marxism. These problems, of the part played in human actions, and the determination of social events, by material and/or ideological factors are central to socialist feminism (see Taylor 1983; Weir and Wilson 1984).

The various interpretations of *The Origin* offered here, and existing elsewhere, all attest to the vitality of the debates within feminism about the determining effects of ideology and of the material world in the construction of women's subordination. But as is often the case with writing on texts, their exposition tells more about the theoretical position of the commentator than about the writer of the original text. De Beauvoir, for example, reveals more about herself than she does about Engels in discussing his work. The lack of interest in Engels of many bourgeois and radical feminists may reflect the difference between their attitude and that of Engels to the socially problematic issue of private property. Equally, the recent popularity of Engels with feminist anthropologists (Kathleen Gough, Karen Sachs etc.) may arise from the promise which Engels seems to offer of a transcultural explanation of sexual subordination – an explanation which then lends itself to the possibility of feminist internationalism.

These uses and abuses of Engels, and shifts and ambivalences within socialism and feminism, are all fully reflected in this collection. In the opening chapter Jane Humphries draws attention to the hostility of many feminists towards *The Origin* – a hostility she locates in a reading of Engels which interprets the book as reducing sexual inequality and the sexual division of labour to nothing more than the results of class divisions in production and private property. She points out that feminists have variously inverted Engels' thesis – arguing that class inequality is determined by sex inequality – or argued that production and reproduction should be treated as relatively autonomous. Starting from the failure of Engels' analysis to explain the persistence of the working-class family (whereas it is relatively successful in explaining propertied family forms), she suggests that sexual divisions in the family and in social production can be better explained as an effect not of wealth but of scarcity – something that is determined by the interplay of production and reproduction. These sexual divisions, she suggests, have developed as a means whereby the family supervises relations between the sexes so as to ensure that children are not produced until they can be catered for at as good, or at a higher, standard of living than they themselves enjoy. As evidence she cites the relatively high levels of illegitimacy occurring where divisions of labour between the sexes are minimal.

Martha Gimenez, like Jane Humphries, also starts with the recent tendency in feminism to treat the family and reproduction as relatively autonomous from production. She suggests that this tendency also characterized *The Origin*, in so far as Engels there treats the family of his time and its supposed unchanging 'battle of the sexes' as eternal – thereby explaining sexual inequality in abstract and idealist rather than materialist terms. This included his explaining it in terms of men's will to dominate over women for the purposes of ensuring the entailment of their property to their biological heirs – an explanation that, in common with some recent feminist explanations of sex inequality, concerns itself with the manifest appearance of relations between the sexes rather than with the underlying structures of the mode of production that determines these relations, their psychology, and their superstructural appearance and effects.

On the other hand, as she also shows, in so far as Engels adopted Marx's method of historical materialism he thereby enables us to conceptualize this underlying structure, revealing the way the 'battle of the sexes' is historically produced through the articulation over time of relations of production and reproduction. In this, her paper constitutes a theoretical supplement to that of Jane Humphries, for this shows the way this articulation operated in the working class of feudal and industrializing England in the determination of conditions of scarcity and in the regulation of relations between the sexes so as to secure the best means of dealing with these conditions.

Following on from this, Janet Sayers also discusses the contribution made by *The Origin* to our understanding of variation in family forms. She shows how Engels demonstrated the nineteenth-century form of the family, taken by his contemporaries (and sometimes by Engels himself) to be eternal and unchanging, to have been the product of, and in turn to have been changed by the contradictions that exist between the forces and relations of production. She goes on to examine the ways in which feminists have recently resorted to psychoanalysis to explain the psychological effects of current inequalities between the sexes. Going beyond these uses of psychoanalysis, she argues that Freud's work provides a useful addition to Engels' *The Origin* in describing the subjective, as distinct from the objective effects of the contradictory forces standing in the way of the realization of 'individual sex love' – forces that Engels located as deriving principally from the institution of private property.

It is this aspect of *The Origin* – specifically Engels' assumption that once property is socialized individual sex love will come into its own, thereby liberating women as well as men – that is taken up and criticized by Mary Evans. As she indicates, this leads Engels to overlook the fact that as women do not necessarily gain as men do from the liberalization of individual sex love – at least in the patriarchal form in which Engels conceptualized it – it is little wonder that the transition to socialism has not brought about full equality and improvement of personal and private relations between the sexes. Engels' ideals of individual sex love and of the family reflect the patriarchal ideology of his age. This is particularly unfortunate in that it means that feminists cannot find in Engels an account of the family and its optimal transformation – one which takes account of its caring as well as of its loving aspects – with which to counter the idealization of the family and of women's subordinate status in it now so successfully promulgated by the Right.

Nevertheless, as Moira Maconachie indicates, feminists and socialists have regularly looked on *The Origin* as a useful counter to right-wing idealization of the bourgeois family as essentially constant and eternal. She goes on to point out that the universalization of this family form and of existing relations between the sexes that Martha and Mary show also to characterize Engels' work, results from Engels treating these relations at one and the same time both as historically produced and mutable, and as fixed by nature. His naturalistic account of the division of labour between the sexes – of women's supposed biologically-given tasks in the home as the original source of their not contributing as men do to social production – is contradicted, she says, by ethnographic and sociological data showing that women regularly contribute to subsistence activity and to social production, albeit this contribution is structured by the sexual divisions of family life. It was Engels' neglect of this that led him to overlook the fact that women's entry into social production could not of itself transform relations between the sexes, that this depends on the transformation of sexual divisions within the family as well as outside society – a condition of women's emancipation that cannot adequately be theorized in the naturalistic terms in which Engels explains sexual divisions within the family.

Nanneke Redclift further explores the enthnographic and anthropological questions mentioned in the previous chapter. She starts with the observation that, because many feminists feel incompetent to judge the accuracy of Engels' anthropology, they overlook ethnographic evidence on the cross-cultural variation in relations between the sexes that might otherwise correct the all too persistent tendency in feminism to treat present relations between the sexes as static and unchanging. She then goes on to consider developments in anthropology since Engels, pointing out that Morgan's work initiated a tradition in anthropology which prioritized kinship as an object of analysis. In the ensuing debate about the material and social determinants of kinship its biological connotations were challenged, but the political nature of sexual divisions that had been an important aspect of Engels' use of Morgan's work on kinship became marginal. Although concern with gender categories is fundamental to the work of Lévi-Strauss, his treatment of kinship as a communication system, and of men and women as mere signs within this system and its exchanges, failed to explain the material aspects of the inequalities in social power between the sexes in kinship exchange.

In contrast, Marxist anthropologists such as Meillasoux do deal with such factors but, in treating women as mere means of reproduction, lose sight of women's agency in social relations. Nanneke Redclift concludes by showing how more justice is done to women as agents as well as subjects in social interaction by an analysis of the ways in which particular cultural systems construct the interplay between power, gender, and kinship, and give symbolic meaning to the processes through which control of rights in reproduction is assured.

While, as this chapter demonstrates, anthropology has barely engaged with the important issues raised for feminism by *The Origin*, this can hardly be said of the Communist Party in the People's Republic of China where, as Delia Davin notes, the book has been one of the major texts used to influence and legitimize socialist thinking, practice and policy about the family and work, divorce and woman's employment. Delia shows how, in the last sixty years in China, the radical message of Engels' *The Origin* has been tailored to make it more acceptable to the patriarchal concerns of the peasantry — an accommodation that is coming under particular strain today when its 1884 Preface is now being pressed into service to justify China's one-child policy. That is, Delia ends with the point with which Jane begins this book, namely with the way that limitations and scarcity of economic resources resulting from particular conjunctions of the relations of production and reproduction affect the regulation – whether by family or state – of relations between the sexes and their reproduction; a point that draws on Engels' *The Origin* and at the same time goes beyond it. And, of course, the issue of the relation of reproduction and production, of patriarchy and capitalism, of sex and class, also continues to be central to the theory and practice of the women's movement in the West, where these aspects of social life are variously treated as interdependent 'fragments' or as separate and distinct sites of struggle (Rowbotham 1979). It is therefore not for nothing that Engels' account in the 1884 Preface of the relation of production and reproduction constitutes the major unifying theme of the following papers, some of which were first presented at the University of Kent in a conference held in May 1984 to commemorate the centenary of the first publication of *The Origin*. The editors would like to thank all those who took part on that occasion for their stimulating and constructive presentation of differing viewpoints, and for generating the enthusiasm which has provided the impetus for this collection.

References

Althusser, L. (1970) *For Marx*. London: New Left Books.

Draper, H. and Lipow, A.G. (1976) Marxist women versus bourgeois feminism. In R. Miliband and J. Saville (eds) *The Socialist Register*. London: Merlin Press.

Engels, F. (1890) *Karl Marx and Frederick Engels: Selected Works*. Moscow: Progress Publishing. (1971 edn.) Letter to J. Bloch in Königsberg (p. 682).

Le Doeuff, M. (1980) Simone de Beauvoir and existentialism. *Feminist Studies* 6(2):277–89.

Lenin, V.I. (1919) *The State*. Peking: Foreign Languages Press.

Luxemburg, R. (1912) Women's suffrage and class struggle. In D. Howard (ed.) *Selected Political Writings of Rosa Luxemburg*. New York: Monthly Review Press (1971 edn.).

Millett, K. (1971) *Sexual Politics*. New York: Avon.

Pollitt, H. (1950) Foreword. *Women and Communism*. London: Lawrence & Wishart.

Porter, C. (1980) *Alexandra Kollontai: A Biography*. London: Virago.
Rowbotham, S. (1973) *Hidden from History*. London: Pluto Press.
—— (1979) The women's movement and organising for socialism. In S.
    Rowbotham, L. Segal, and H. Wainwright (eds) *Beyond the Fragments*.
    London: Merlin Press.
Taylor, B. (1983) *Eve and the New Jerusalem*. London: Virago.
Thönnessen, W. (1973) *The Emancipation of Women*. (Translated by Joris de
    Bres.) London: Pluto Press.
Vogel, L. (1983) *Marxism and the Oppression of Women* London: Pluto Press.
Weir, A. and Wilson, E. (1984) The British women's movement. *New Left
    Review* 148 (Nov./Dec.):74–103.
Lu, Yu-Lan *et al* (1972) *New Women in New China*. Peking: Foreign
    Languages Press.

2

The origin of the family: Born out of scarcity not wealth

Jane Humphries

Introduction:

Engels' book, *The Origin of the Family, Private Property and the State* (1884) stands in somewhat ambiguous regard with contemporary feminists. On the one hand it identifies and examines issues which are central to feminism: the origin of the family and the nature and meaning of women's oppression. Furthermore it employs a method of analysis which should be applauded as a pathbreaking attempt to develop a feminist methodology in the sense that human reproduction is identified along with production as constituting the material basis of society. Thus, contrary to some inaccurately hostile interpretations, Engels views activities concerned with reproduction as analytically equivalent to those concerned with production in the understanding of human society.

On the other hand, the execution of the analysis is less than perfect. In particular there is slippage between the status of human reproduction in Engels' exposition of his approach and its role in the actual analysis. From a feminist perspective this constitutes a fatal flaw. As human reproduction slides out of the material base, its organization becomes dependent on the organization of production. Hence feminist issues become secondary, and the contradiction between men and women subservient to that between capital and labour. Not surprisingly feminists regard as specious Engels' conclusion that the material basis of women's oppression lies in the same institution as the material basis of class oppression, and are suspicious of a derivative politics which identifies women's struggle with the class struggle. For the latter, which they recognize as the focal point of Marxist analysis and Marxist politics, is bound to dominate.

Consequently, feminist authors, particularly those struggling to escape from what they regard as the chauvinist constraints of classical Marxism, have engaged in a certain amount of Engels 'bashing'. The latter has, on occasion, amounted to rather unfair castigation of Engels for failing to develop feminist theory in ways which would have been entirely alien, while simultaneously not recognizing that the object of their scorn occupies this position precisely because of his, by contemporary if not modern standards, sensitivity to feminist issues.

Meanwhile the development of anthropology has cast important doubts on the validity of Morgan's research and hence the empirical support for Engels' vision of family organization in societies which were not characterized by private property. Although we still read Engels and refer to *The Origin*, modern feminists essentially use it as a straw man whose complacent and inaccurate prognostication provides a useful counterpoise to our own more sophisticated analysis.

The purposes of this chapter are twofold. First, prompted by the occasion of the conference, I argue that *The Origin* does contain the germ of a feminist methodology which subsequently has been developed (albeit in different ways) by many authors. In the following section I discuss the essential points of Engels' theorization of the family in capitalism and the transition to capitalism, avoiding the anthropological debate (on which I am not qualified to comment) and arguing that they retain considerable explanatory power. Further, if one crucial change in Engels' argument is made, its usefulness is seen to increase dramatically.

Engels' methodology: Its problems and its potential

Marx and Engels claimed that 'men must be in a position to live in order to make history' and that 'life involves before everything else eating, drinking, a habitation, clothing and many other things' (Marx and Engels 1845:30). It is fundamental to a Marxist approach that this physiological priority translates into material determination, that is that the way in which the fundamental necessities needed to sustain life are produced constitutes the material basis of society and that this is, in the well worn Marxist phrase, 'determinant in the last instance'. The exact meaning of this phrase has, of course, promoted endless controversy within Marxism. But this is not particularly important here. While my interpretation is that the prior necessity of material production does endow it with determining power in the shaping of the social whole, it is enough for our purposes if a weaker premise is accepted: simply that the importance of production is such that it provides a useful entry point into social analysis, a good way to start to unravel the interconnected relationships which comprise the social whole. All this is rather familiar terrain.

Less fully appreciated is Marx's and Engels' insistence that '[Another] circumstance which from the very outset enters into historical development, is that men, who daily remake their own life begin to make other men, to propagate their kind' (Marx and Engels 1845:31). This clear location of human reproduction and the social relations of human reproduction in the material base of the society recurs in Marx's writing on precapitalist modes of production (Marx 1857–58:83) and in Engels' *The Origin*. Indeed the latter contains one of the clearest statements locating human reproduction in the material base and therefore assigning to the family a key role in the total organization of society: 'The social organization under which the people of a particular historical epoch and a particular country live is determined by both kinds of production: by the stage of development of labour on the one hand and of the family on the other' (Engels 1884:72).

For Engels the latter involves the physical reproduction of living human beings but must also include the nurturing and sustenance of the young, as it is adults capable of both labour and procreation who must be reproduced. Historically this process has taken place in the context of the family. The latter also bears some responsibility for 'socialization', that is the process by which human beings are invested with the willingness to work, bear children, and generally support the social relations characteristic of the existing society. But this responsibility is shared with other institutions, such as the schools, the church, the media, etc., partly or wholly concerned with the reproduction of existing social relations, that is, *social* reproduction. However intertwined in everyday life, the family's ideological functions are theoretically distinguishable from the material practice of human reproduction.

Engels was insistent that historical analysis must emphasize the interaction between these *two* aspects of material life, that is between the changing organization of production and the changing form of the family. But in his study Engels failed to keep human reproduction and material production analytically separate, because in many precapitalist economies kinship relations structure both human reproduction and material production, i.e. the family is the unit of both reproduction and production (Meillasoux 1975). As a result Engels' historical analysis neglects human reproduction as a relatively autonomous structure and his discussion of the family is subsumed under his discussion of the mode of production.

For example, in his famous 'explanation' of the institution of monogamy, Engels described the emergence of transferable wealth in the form of herds of animals as strengthening the relative position of men within the family and leading to the overthrow of matrilinearity, the hitherto traditional order of inheritance. Given the possibility of bequests, monogamy was then instituted in order to ensure paternity.

There have been several well founded criticisms of this analysis. Why herds should be distinguished from older forms of property is not explained. Tools, for example, had simply been bequeathed to members of the tribe of the same sex, and, since they did not seem to have been 'owned' in any privatistic sense, appear to have been undisruptive of the ancient egalitarianism of the *gens* (Sacks 1975). Nor is it clear why men controlled the herds when agricultural subsistence production was women's sphere. If when the wealth was produced it was wrested from women's control, men must already have appropriated power (Lane 1976).

But from the critical perspective developed here it is more unfortunate that in Engels' analysis changes in the form of the family are determined by changes in the relations of material production as reflected in changes in property forms. The development of the production capacity of labour, reflected in the growth of herds, 'explains' not only the transition to monogamy but also the abandonment of matrilinearity which together symbolize changes in the structure of reproduction that have disastrous effects on the social position of women. 'The man took command in the home also; the woman was degraded and reduced to servitude. She became the slave of his lust and a mere instrument for the production of children' (Engels 1884:120–21). Monogamy for Engels had nothing to do with love or affection but was simply a means to protect and to concentrate wealth (1884:128).

Woman's specialization in the home now increasingly worked against her. The decline of subsistence production and the growth of production centres outside the home weakened the woman's position ever further because it undermined her ability to contribute directly to her family's well-being.

Thus Engels attributes the *origin* of the monogamous family and the origin of male dominance over women to the emergence of private property. Hence women's oppression is linked to the emergence of socioeconomic classes, for with private property came differences in wealth and social standing.

But in the course of this analysis Engels violates the schema outlined earlier which depicted reproduction as a second autonomous, if interrelated, moment of the material. Instead the family form and the relationship between the sexes is structured by the organization of production. Feminists have been rightly suspicious of both the theoretical reduction of their main concerns and the derived politics which, without contradiction, identifies women's struggle with struggle against private property and therefore struggle against capital. For these and related reasons many feminists reject Marxist theory as inappropriate, as, in effect, obfuscation of the real contradiction between men and women. But even among those feminists who purport to reject the classical Marxist approach to the woman question, its influence is unmistakable. Firestone, for example, proposes an inversion of Marx's framework, with the contradiction between the sexes *replacing* that between the classes (Firestone 1974). Similarly, Christine Delphy's attempt to establish a materialist feminism, while formally differentiated from Marxism, relies on Marx's concept of exploitation identified with the extraction of surplus labour, only in Delphy's analysis men appropriate the labour time of women rather than capitalists appropriating the labour time of workers (Delphy 1977, 1980).

These 'radical' feminist writings can be seen to develop a form of analysis in which society is conceptualized as consisting of two separate structures variously described as: the economic class system/the sex class system (e.g. Firestone); the industrial mode of production/the family mode of production (e.g. Delphy); capitalism/patriarchy (e.g. Hartmann 1979; Eisenstein 1979; Ferguson and Folbre 1981). The contribution of the radical feminists has been to reject the tendency, inherited from Marx's and Engels' practice, if not from their theoretical framework, to *reduce* these structures to a unitary whole dominated by the economic class system/industrial mode of production/capitalism. In reaction, however, they overemphasized the autonomy of both the economy and the family as distinct separate determinants of historical change and indeed, in the cases cited above, reversed the Marxist error by seemingly accepting a hierarchy of determination only with the sex class system now pre-eminent.

Reacting both to the initial disappointment with the classical Marxist approach and to the radical critique, many feminist writers have sought to conceptualize the interaction and interrelationship between these two structures, a problem exacerbated both by their imbrication and by the difficulties of definition experienced with respect to the sex class system/family mode of production/ patriarchy (Beechey 1979; Edholm, Harris, and Young 1977; Barrett 1980). Although the terminology is not uniform and the hierarchies of gender and class have not yet been satisfactorily linked, the view that the family and the economy are *relatively* autonomous and equivalent in analytic status would appear to be the dominant one emerging from this debate (Kuhn and Wolpe

1978; Beechey 1979; Barrett 1980; Humphries and Rubery 1984). The similarity between this conceptualization and that originally proposed by Marx and especially Engels in *The Origin* is striking. But the problem of how to develop this theoretical insight remains. We have seen that despite their good intentions Marx and Engels slid into economic determinism in their historical analysis. Modern radical feminists in reaction seem to have inverted their mistake. The difficulty here is that a methodological position which denies functionalism and hierarchy in determination, which demands a careful analysis of interacting structures, and which stresses the uniqueness of historical conjunctures, cannot produce dramatic general statements. It demands instead detailed empirical analyses of the interactions between these key structures and the implications of the adaptions and antagonisms for other aspects of the social structure, work which has recently been (in my view) misleading represented as '[placing] us firmly back on the terrain of empirical sociology' (Brenner and Ramas 1984:34). But whatever the difficulties of developing such a 'dual system' approach, to pose the issue in this way illustrates the relationship between much contemporary feminist writing and the approach proposed if not pursued by Marx and Engels. It also suggests the enormous amount of work involved in feminist progress.

The family in capitalism: Its origin and meaning

We have seen that although physical reproduction was recognized as a moment of the material and understood as structuring family relations, the latter's simultaneous constitution of relations of production within capitalist modes of production distracted both Marx and Engels. Emphasis was on the family as the unit of production in the pre-capitalist economy and on changes in family forms as determined by the laws of motion of material production. In short the material base of the family was collapsed into the mobilization, concentration and intergenerational transfer of property. This is the essence concealed by the appearance of family affection, conjugal love, blood ties and so on.

Marx's and Engels' theorization of the family in capitalism is directly derived. Significantly it is a class-differentiated theory. The proleteriat is by definition propertyless. What need then for a mechanism for the concentration and inheritance of property? In precapitalism, family relations had facilitated the organization of the labour process and the productive mobilization of property to which the direct producers frequently retained access even after property rights had been lost. With capitalism production moved outside the home and was concentrated and centralized in the factory system. So capitalist accumulation 'breaks up the family'.

References to the 'abolition of the working-class family' carefully interwoven with supportive contemporary social commentary are ubiquitous in Marx's and Engels' writings. Engels, for example, concludes his documentation of the traumatic effects of early capitalist industrialism on working-class family life with the following:

> 'Such a state of affairs [i.e. the decay of family life] shows clearly that this is no rational or sensible principle at the root of our ideas concerning family income and property. If the family as it exists in our present society comes to an end then its disappearance will prove that the real bond holding the family together was not affection but merely self-interest engendered by the false concept of family property.' (Engels 1845:168)

Though capitalism is held to destroy the material base of the working-class family it does not have the same effect on the property-owning classes. Early capitalism is characterized by the concentration of wealth within families, the mobilization of family ties to build up business enterprise, and above all the consolidation of the ruling class by intermarriage between the old aristocracy based on the land and the new wealth of trade and industry. Precisely those changes in production depicted as eroding the family among the proletariat fed its survival among the bourgeoisie. But its survival took a distinctly bourgeois form; for Marx, capitalism reduces the family among the propertied classes to a 'dirty existence'. Productive aspects that had survived in the elite feudal family are stripped away; all that remains is a 'mere money relation'.

How has this class-differentiated theorization of the family fared in historical analysis? On the one hand the depiction of the family among the property-owning classes appears well supported by what we know about changes in the family in the transition from feudalism to capitalism. The underdeveloped and fragmented feudal economy produced a limited range of forms in which wealth could be held: land, precious metals and inventories of luxury goods whose trade was established, land being by far the most important. Title of ownership of land was generally invested in the ruling aristocracy but the direct producers, in a complex and problematic relationship with the feudal lords, retained access to the land. Control of the agricultural labour process was the prerogative of the village community, heavily influenced by custom and tradition.

Nor was the feudal meaning of ownership limited only by the peasants' rights. Frequently the aristocratic title to land was so legally constrained that the head of the family was reduced to no more than the life tenant of the estates and had no freedom to dispose of them as he wished. These legal arrangements reveal feudal ownership as a 'holy trust' invested in an individual as the representative of his kin, a mystified relationship that sanctified the family estates and prevented their alienation (Stone 1977; Holt 1972).

The legal constraints began to be broken down in the sixteenth century as landowners sought *individualistic* control over their property (Stone 1975). Possibly they hoped to find in the mobilization of their landed wealth new social roles to replace their increasingly defunct military functions, or perhaps the reduced opportunities for younger sons motivated the partition of estates. Whatever the explanation the new more capitalistic notion of 'ownership' (that is that the title was invested in an individual whose rights of disposal were absolute), meant that inheritance was no longer a formality worked through according to custom, tradition, and kin advice. Clearly this increased the power of the head of the household over his wife and children. 'He could not only bribe them with promises of more, he could threaten them with total exclusion from the inheritance' (Stone 1975:36).

More generally, capitalism inaugurated new kinds of private property and, (although not without a struggle), changed the nature of the property forms existing, and transformed attitudes to them. Capitalism, as a mode of material production, is obsessed like no other with the notion of property. Reflecting this, postmedieval, and perhaps more intensively eighteenth-century, British legal history can be read as the redefinition of 'property' and 'ownership', backed up by a bloodily repressive penal code and a powerful legal ideology, a redefinition which not incidentally secured a redistribution of national resources in favour of those doing the defining (Hay *et al.* 1975; Thompson 1976; Kiernan 1976).

The liberation of the disposition of property from the jurisdiction of custom, as already hinted, was paralleled by a simultaneous decline in the importance of the kin group relative to the nuclear family and an aggrandizement of the male head of household (the property owner) within that nuclear family. The new massive presence of property also enhanced the importance of the institution closely connected with the management concentration and alliance of fortunes – marriage. Medieval marriage had been primarily an instrument for building up political alliances between specific groups or individuals and occasionally replenishing the fortune of some elite family that had either gentility or political clout to exchange. Increasingly, with the rise of the absolute state and the decay of *feudal* power, along with the development of trade and industry, the political motive became subsidiary to the economic motive. Seventeenth, eighteenth, and nineteenth-century marriage was accompanied by detailed financial settlement which provided the best lawyers with a good part of their fees (Hay *et al.* 1975; Stone 1977; and see also Habakkuk 1940).

Even the divisions noted among the ruling class were vulnerable to the bridge of matrimony. A casual inspection of the literature of the period illustrates the social importance of affinity and reflects the frequency with which the marriage settlement was the sacrament by which land allied itself with trade and later industry. The network of marriage ties served to soften the distinctions between the ruling groups and prevent dangerous divisions from widening. For example, the early alliances between landed families and the rising commercial interests served to consolidate and link old political authority with new economic power. 'The landed gentry absorbed commercial capital through inter-marriage and invested passively in commercial ventures, but their main assets lay in land and office. They used their status and political power to create wealth whereas merchants created wealth in order to purchase influence and prestige' (Grassby 1970:107; and see Landes 1975).

For any individual merchant a tie to the land was a way of moving out of highly liquid assets (that could readily be dissipated by his heirs) into a more permanent form of wealth and thereby protecting future generations from an occasional family dissolute. Not surprisingly, many marriage settlements by merchants insisted that land be purchased (Grassby 1977).

It follows from the above that marriage was frequently the instrument whereby surplus realized in one sector was transferred into another (Cottrell 1980:3). Much has been made about the movement into land of profits realized in unequal exchange, but as a counterpoise much early industrial investment was financed out of agricultural profits built up over generations. The finance for Oldham's early cotton mills has been described as the product of kulak practices: 'Careful marriage, sharp bargaining, tenancy in common' (Foster 1974:12).

Not only the nuclear family but also the broader kinship ties retained an economic importance after their significance as a political micro-system had been overshadowed by the growth of other loyalties (Stone 1975). Among the commercial community, kinship ties were important from the sixteenth century onwards as a source of loans, partnership investments, and agencies for job placement (Cottrell 1980; Mathias 1983; Landes 1975). Given that it was not until the eighteenth century that judges at last created a coherent legal framework for commerce, and even their legal protection was far from perfect, it is easy to see why the additional trust that a tie of blood or marriage implied would be valued. Nor were the benefits confined to commercial ventures. The Lees and the Cleggs, two of the largest employers in the early cotton industry, were really kinship alliances, the individual component families bound together by a whole system of joint business ventures (Foster 1974:12).

Engels' economism fares less well when attention is turned to the working-class family. Although affected by capitalism in terms both of structure and function, the working-class family has certainly not 'withered away'. Moreover its resilience relates not only to the imperatives of accumulation, but also to the structures of defensive and even aggressive struggles waged by the working class. These arguments are well known (Humphries 1977; Rubery 1978; Grieco and Whipp 1984; Humphries and Rubery 1984). A further critical dimension is revealed if the issue is re-examined within Engels' original framework.

Human reproduction requires, as its essential condition of existence, heterosexual adult relationships. The very obviousness of this has been problematic. Heterosexuality has been understood as 'natural' and 'innate' even though this flies in the face not only of scientific practice but also of established evidence. Anthropologists have documented the heterogeneity of encountered forms of human sexuality, and the evidence from psychoanalytic clinical findings indicates that there is nothing inevitable or pre-established in the development of human sexuality. The assumption that heterosexuality is natural and therefore normal is clearly related to its function as a condition of existence of reproduction viewed from a strongly evolutionary if unconscious value system (Chodorow 1978; Gimenez 1980).

While the implications of heterosexuality for the differentiation between the sexes and the creation of gender via the specific and systematic interpretation of those differences has been a major concern to feminists, the point here is that reproduction has its own imperative involving the generation of aggressive heterosexuality. What are the implications for the interaction between reproduction and production?

Preindustrial Europe generally had high levels of mortality. Mere stability of population required that birth rates be high (Laslett 1965; Laslett and Wall 1972). Heterosexuality becomes the norm precisely because it secures reproduction in such a hostile environment (Gimenez 1980). Other forms of sexuality were luxuries which a society ravaged by plagues and pestilence, characterized by high infant mortality and short life expectancy, could not afford to regard as other than deviant.

Historically, except for some very privileged communities in isolated times and places, the key characteristic of most economies has been *scarcity*: albeit a scarcity which is more or less intense and differently distributed according to the dominant mode of production. At any point in time the productive potential of any specific historical economy has been limited. At the micro level this is experienced in the struggle, more or less intense, to survive (Laslett 1965; Clark 1968; Wilson 1984; Hutchins 1915). Over time, that is intergenerationally, this means that families cannot produce unlimited numbers of children without involving themselves and their children in deteriorating standards, which in the context of historic poverty may deny survival. Deterioration in standards of living for the property-owning classes and aristocracy or peasantry translates into the parcellation of property and the fragmentation of holdings (Foster and Ranum 1976; Goody, Thirsk, and Thompson 1976). Hence, in these classes, *property* appears as the material foundation of the family. But the general case is one not of *wealth* but of *scarcity*.

Putting these arguments together: the contention here is that the insistent socialization into heterosexuality has stood in explosive contradiction with economic scarcity. Given that the latter is (i) more or less chronic depending on the development of the forces of production, and (ii) within any particular society will be differentially experienced by the different classes, the contradiction itself will be mediated by the mode of production and class location. But the resolution, or at least management, of this contradiction is the primary function of the family *in all classes*. Thus the family as a structure derives from neither production nor reproduction but from the tense interface between the two.

The family emerges historically as the institution which regulates relationships between the sexes, particularly in their fecund youth, organizes intercourse and marriage, and imposes celibacy and singleness.

Much historical work on the family is relevant to this interpretation, but rather than survey this now enormous secondary
literature it will be more interesting to focus on one outstanding
issue: the role of women.

In early capitalist and late feudal economies, most women had to
contribute to production because given the levels of labour
productivity and the rate of exploitation there was no possibility of
survival via income pooling (Clark 1968; Hutchins 1915; Pinchbeck
1969; Richards 1974). Simultaneously mothers' special role in
human reproduction differentiated their tasks (for a more standard
interpretation here see Beneria 1979, and for a recent reemphasis on
biology, which is, incidentally, developed in a framework which
seems ultimately to return to the dual systems theoretical approach
which they reject, see Brenner and Ramas 1984). Not so much the
bearing of children but their successful rearing required close
contacts between a mother and her child during its infancy.
Modern research (UNICEF 1983) confirms fragmentary historical
evidence (Acton 1859; Wray 1978; Knodel and Van de Walle 1967;
McLauren 1977) suggesting that breast feeding was the key to
infant survival in the absence of facilities for bottle feeding,
sterilization equipment, appropriate feeds, pure water, etc.

Most married women in the childbearing ages would be either
breast feeding or pregnant, which clearly compromised the type of
work that they could do. They either had to carry the baby with
them, which was likely to erode productivity in tasks involving
simultaneously moving around geographically; or they had to
work close to their settlement so that they were readily accessible.
While this is obvious, the more difficult question is how a division
of labour involving some *subgroup* of the female workforce became
generalized even at the expense of misallocation.

The universality of a sexual division of labour has been
something of an enigma. Feminists, quite rightly, have criticized
The Origin for its obliviousness to the implications for hierarchy
and oppression of specialization in production.

Here the new framework proves useful. Remember that the
family has to regulate and supervise contacts between the young of
different sexes including their interaction while at work. The

difficulties of combining effective supervision with concentrated labour promoted solutions which circumscribed *the framework* within which contact occurred. The first solution lay in *family labour*; that is, the employment of the reproductive unit as a production unit with limited contact with other labour units, and tight reins on contacts with other individuals. This reconciliation of the demands of production with the control of reproduction, while not ideally suited to some tasks where the age and sex composition of the optimal labour force diverged from the age and sex composition of a 'normal' family, was readily adapted to other tasks, especially to the characteristic early industrial combination of domestic industry with some agricultural by-employment and/or home production. Once in place, family labour systems developed with the evolving mode of production and were readily integrated with wage labour (Medick 1976; Anderson 1971; Smelser 1959; Humphries 1981). Their popularity in time and space testifies to their successful mediation of family needs with the demands of the labour process.

But controlling cross-sex contacts was much easier in the *context of a sexual division of labour*. Hence the characteristic feature of the late medieval and early capitalist labour process: men and women did not work together except as family members. Exceptions to this rule were well publicized and denounced as socially disruptive. As with family labour, once affirmed, the sexual division of labour developed in tandem with the mode of production. In particular it becomes part of the arena of struggle not only between the direct producers and those owning the means of production, but also between fragmented capital and divided workers. An existing sexual division of labour may derive support from the practices of monopsonistic employers, and male-dominated trade unions as well as historically established social conventions.

It is not only a major project to develop the empirical evidence supportive of the hypothesis developed here, but one singularly unsuited to this occasion. It is however appropriate to list, in varying degrees of detail, some areas of historical controversy where a framework which emphasizes the tension between scarcity and heterosexuality seems useful.

The first topic is that of the documentation and discussion of the sexual division of labour itself. It has been impossible to explain the breadth and depth of the sexual division of labour by reference to different physical capabilities for it is well known that women's work historically has been as gruelling and laborious as that of men (Clark 1968; Pinchbeck 1969; Alexander 1976).

Nor is adequate explanation forthcoming from the constraint of childbearing. Sexual differentiation has always extended beyond the tasks which might functionally be related to the former, even extended to include nursing, into domesticity more broadly defined, and has also applied to all women, not only those who were currently bearing children: points which are not convincingly explained by, for example, Brenner and Ramas's recent presentation of the sexual division of labour as emerging 'from the confrontation between the demands of capitalist accumulation and the structures of human reproduction' (Brenner and Ramas 1984:71). These puzzling aspects of the sexual division of labour are better understood if it is interpreted, as above, as a framework within which the family sought to control the sexual and reproductive behaviour of its (particularly junior) members. Then the constraints of childbearing, and more important historically breastfeeding, on the geographical mobility of mothers promoted a specialization in domesticity which was extended by the need to control and supervise the behaviour of unmarried women and girls into a *comprehensive* sexual division of labour. Young women, simply because they needed to be under the watchful eyes of an older female relative who was already likely to be constrained by her reproductive responsibilities, were directed to the same arenas and tasks as their mothers and grandmothers. To the extent that the latter provided sufficient outlet for the labour of the women of the family, control involved little economic sacrifice. But for families with large numbers of daughters, and/or with reduced scope to utilize labour on the domestic front (absence of cottage industry, reduced access to land, etc.) the costs could be higher. In these circumstances the traditional standards were probably violated. Furthermore the pressures on any individual family from the broader economic context, whether this be feudal or capitalist, could strain the sexual division of labour.

Interesting supportive evidence here is provided by Christopher Middleton's observation of a clear sexual division of labour among unfree wage workers in feudal England in contrast to the sharing of tasks by peasants of both sexes working their own land (Middleton 1979). As these workers were least likely to be married Middleton sees this as at odds with a biological interpretation of the sexual division of labour: 'For if occupational inequalities were a direct consequence of differences in biological function, then we would expect those women who were married and most frequently subject to the demands of bearing and nursing children to suffer most from the sexual division of labour' (Middleton 1979:167).

With the development of the economy, and in particular the declining opportunities for productively combining substantive amounts of female labour with other resources within the domestic arena, the costs of this form of social control escalated. This translates into the widely held view that the transition to capitalism involved declining opportunities for women to contribute to family income (Pinchbeck 1969; Snell 1981). The institution of family labour provided a solution which was widely exploited during the transitional period (Smelser 1959; Anderson 1971; Clark 1968; Humphries 1981). The putting out of industrial tasks, based on an at least partially captive pool of female labour, was another structural accommodation to the segmentation of the labour supply inherited from the earlier mode of production. But with declining opportunities for whole families to work together (Smelser 1959; Levine 1977; Humphries 1981) along with reduced scope for women to contribute to family income without recourse to wage labour, the strain between these traditional frameworks for social control and the demands of the developing capitalist economy deepened. In the interim control weakened, as indirectly indicated by the rising incidence of illegitimacy in the 1700s (Shorter 1971; Laslett, Oosterveen, and Smith 1980).

While a new equilibrium of social convention emerged to reduce the risks of thoughtless and improvident relationships, and one which of necessity crystallized the sexual division of labour within waged work, with increased wage dependence the life cycle of income experienced by families changed and for brief periods of time the prospects of men and women who had no productive resources other than their own labour power appeared rosier than ever. Old income strategies regarding marriage and childbearing looked outdated and behaviour changed (McLauren 1977). This was reflected in changes in the age of marriage, in the proportions marrying, and ultimately in population growth (Laslett and Wall 1972; Levine 1977; Levine 1985).

To summarize: first, the argument developed here is supported by the sexual divisions of labour observed in late feudal England; second, it provides a new way of interpreting the evidence that the transition to capitalism had adverse effects on women workers; and, third, it informs hypothesized links between structural changes in the economy and changes in demographic indicators. Furthermore, an emphasis on the social control implicit in the sexual division of labour also explains the frequency with which, historically, sex segmentation was rationalized and justified by references to decency and morality, a point to which we now turn.

Historians have often been surprised by eighteenth and nineteenth-century social commentators' obsession with the sexual standards and behaviour of their subjects (Thompson and Yeo 1973; Razzell and Wainwright 1973; Humphries 1981). The framework proposed here motivates this concern by linking sexual license with potential, if not actual, children whose parents were unlikely to be able to support them and who therefore represented a palpable burden on kin more broadly defined (particularly the mothers' parents) and residually, given the local organization of social welfare (The Old and New Poor Laws), on the community. The implications of this for analysis of the development of popular morality in relation to the relevant ideological state apparatuses of the eighteenth and nineteenth centuries are very interesting, particularly when the relationship is also located in a developing capitalist economy. It may well be that researchers anxious to understand the characteristics of mature variants of women's subordination (sexual division of labour in paid work, wage differentials, sexual division of labour between paid and unpaid work, sexual harassment particularized in time and place, etc.)

might be persuaded to consider not only the specific returns such treatment of women provides to men, but also its links to a past burdened with scarcity and driven by heterosexuality. Indeed in a sense this framework comes right back to Engels' original intended research: to combine an understanding of both reproduction and production as moments of the material in the particular context of women's subordination.

It might be helpful to try to illustrate these points by reference to a historical issue on which I am currently working: the incidence and significance of illegitimacy. It was implied above that illegitimacy indicated a failure of the social control of fertility. The argument is that illegitimate children were illegitimate *because* there was no economic space for them, rather than that there was no economic space for them because they were illegitimate. Illegitimate children were children whose births were not only unplanned but whose existence could not be supported. Premarital pregnancy was another issue, often readily accommodated by subsequent marriage. Bastards' parents could not or would not marry. Overwhelmingly this was because of their material circumstances which, in turn, inhibited the prospects of the unfortunate children. Look at the hard realities of life for illegitimate children: even by the late nineteenth century their chances of survival were only half as good as those of legitimate children (Farr 1885), the more dramatic threat of infanticide overshadowed in reality by the economic disadvantages endemic to their status. And they were highly likely to be reduced to dependence on the Poor Law, often within the hated workhouses. According to the Webbs, between 1834 and 1908 some one-third of all individuals afforded Poor Relief were children, and tens of thousands of those in the workhouses were foundlings and orphans, the majority of the former being illegitimate (Webb and Webb 1929).

Significantly, the history of the laws on bastardy, at least as interpreted for the Poor Law Commissioners in 1840 by Sir Edmund Head, involved 'no trace of . . . enactments for the punishment of seduction . . . and . . . compassionate regard for the frailty of the weaker sex . . .' (Parliamentary Papers 1840:83). Instead Sir Edmund found legislation which was 'Unsparing on the woman [which] we might have attributed to a zeal for morality were it not that its penalties were inflicted not for having the sin of a bastard child but for having a bastard child which may be chargeable to the Parish' (Parliamentary Papers 1840:83). Affiliation was simply one route to privatize the impact of individuals' careless disregard for the consequences of their pleasure and indemnify the parish against the cost of the infant. The Bastardy Clauses of the 1834 Act were a possibly more effective and certainly more misogynist alternative which significantly purported to reduce the alleged incentive to improvident marriage embodied in affiliation; and to replace 'the prop' to women's 'self control' by threatening them with total responsibility for any living product of their shared mistakes. Significantly, too, given our emphasis on familial constraints on individuals' behaviour, the New Poor Law specifically sought to formalize the liability of the mother's *parents*, for as was subsequent remarked 'It seems only reasonable to infer that if they were called upon to pay some small part of the expenses incurred by the parish, they would be led to exercise a more careful supervision over their children's conduct, and thus prevent much after sorrow and disgrace' (Birmingham Ladies Union 1890:138–50).

It follows that the incidence of illegitimacy provides an index of the success of family strategies to control and regulate the demands on resources. Not surprisingly this indicator is known to fluctuate widely. The massive increase in illegitimacy in the early 1600s, for example, clearly signals a breakdown in the equilibrium of controls/regulation and sexuality (Laslett, Oosterveen, and Smith 1980). The usual argument here is that increased mobility and anonymity, in turn derived from economic change, vitiated the community's ability to police contracts, especially implicit contracts, so premarital conception, which in the older stable world would simply have prompted marriage, and been unfortunate but not tragic, now resulted in an illegitimate birth and a permanent strain in the family and/or community involved. But this upsurge was probably also fed by changes in the organization of work which led to greater contacts between men and women. Anyway its resolution clearly had to involve tighter controls and more careful monitoring of contacts if the second-round defence of post-conception marriage could be breached with impunity. Significantly, most empirical evidence suggests a tightening of the sexual division of labour both within ascendant wage labour and between paid and unpaid work. Summaries of the extensive qualitative evidence illustrating these historical trends have already been cited (in particular see Pinchbeck 1969; Snell 1981). The author's own quantitative investigation of census returns reveals a tendency towards increased segmentation that is so consistent across regions as to overcome doubts about the quality of the data involved (Humphries 1984).

It is also interesting that illegitimacy varied dramatically across counties. Explanations have not been very convincing as variation is not readily related to income, age at marriage or religious differences (Leffingwell 1892). The evidence is, however, consistent with the arguments developed here, for the counties with high illegitimacy rates were agrarian/mixed economies with evidence of a less rigorous sexual division of labour. Norfolk, for example, which throughout the eighteenth and nineteenth centuries had a markedly high illegitimacy rate, had a developed system of gang labour which was notorious for the fact that men and women were allowed to work together (Springall 1936; Razzell and Wainwright 1973; Alexander *et al.* 1979).

There are potential counter examples, such as Lancashire, whose specialization in textiles was associated with a high female participation rate and a low degree of sex segmentation in employment, but which had a low incidence of illegitimacy throughout the nineteenth century. However Lancashire's early factory production was mediated first through a family labour system (Smelser 1959) and subsequently characterized by an intra-industry sexual division of labour which is impossible to detect in the crude occupational categories of the early censuses. Moreover the employment of large numbers of women, crowded together by the internal division of labour within factories, has been described as conducive to the diffusion of information about that female method of birth control: abortion (McLauren 1977). Certainly there is evidence that knowledge of abortion was particularly widespread in mid-nineteenth century Lancashire and its practice was cited by contemporaries as an explanation of the low level of illegitimacy in the factory districts (McLauren 1977).

To end with one more illustration: it follows from this model that if the family plays the protective agent in a poor and predatory society, then those who lack this patronage and care run a higher risk of exploitation. Studies of eighteenth and nineteenth-century prostitution suggest that a high proportion of prostitutes were orphans or semi-orphans. Even allowing for systematic upward bias in the reporting of such status the evidence remains convincing (Walkowitz 1980; Parent-Duchâtelet 1836). Similarly the documented existence of a 'bastard bearing subclass' (Laslett, Oosterveen, and Smith 1980) in late medieval and early modern Europe is also readily understood in the framework developed here. Families in this group failed to provide appropriate protection and failed to enforce implicit or tentative contracts. Having failed initially a family lost economically and socially: their cards were subsequently harder to play and their next generation members at greater risk.

Conclusion

It seldom happens, but it is very pleasing when it does, that famous men have tried to live their ideologies. Friedrich Engels was a kind and generous man who tried to develop liberated and liberating relationships with women (Marcus 1974; Kapp 1972). It is thus additionally satisfactory that one hundred years after its publication, and recognizing its drawbacks and deficiencies, feminists still find inspiration and encouragement in *The Origin of the Family, Private Property and the State* as this paper has tried to demonstrate. My guess is that Friedrich Engels himself would have felt very pleased and very honoured.

References

Acton, W. (1859) Observations on illegitimacy in London parishes at St Marylebone, St Pancras and St George's Southwark during the year 1857. *Journal of the Royal Statistical Society* 22.

Alexander S. (1976) Women's work in nineteenth-century London. In J. Mitchell, and A. Oakley (eds) *The Rights and Wrongs of Women*. Harmondsworth: Penguin.

Alexander, S., Davin, A., and Hostettler, E. (1979) Labouring women: A reply to Eric Hobsbawm. *History Workshop* 8.

Anderson, M. (1971) *Family Structure in Nineteenth Century Lancashire*. Cambridge: Cambridge University Press.

Barrett, M. (1980) *Women's Oppression Today*. London: New Left Books.

Beechey, V. (1979) On patriarchy. *Feminist Review* 3.

Beneria, L. (1979) Reproduction, production and the sexual division of labour. *Cambridge Journal of Economics* 3.

Birmingham Ladies Union (1890) Papers read at a conference, Girton College, Cambridge.

Brenner, J. and Ramas, M. (1984) Rethinking women's oppression. *New Left Review* 144.

Clark, A. (1968). *Working Life of Women in the Seventeenth Century*. London: Frank Cass.

Chodorow, N. (1978) *The Reproduction of Mothering*. Berkeley: University of California Press.

Cottrell, P.L. (1980) *Industrial Finance: 1830–1914*. London: Methuen.

Delphy, C. (1977) *The Main Enemy: A Materialist Analysis of Women's Oppression*. London: WRRC Publications. (*Explorations in Feminism* 3).

—— (1980) A materialist feminism is possible. *Feminist Review* 4.

Edholm, F., Harris, O., and Young K. (1977) Conceptualising women. *Critique of Anthropology* 3 (9, 10).

Eisenstein, Z.R. (ed.) (1979) *Capitalist Patriarchy and the Case for Socialist Feminism*. New York: Monthly Review Press.

Engels, F. (1845) *The Condition of the Working-Class in England*. Oxford: Blackwell. (1958 edn.)

—— (1884) *The Origin of the Family, Private Property and the State*. New York: International Publishers. (1972 edn.)

Ferguson, A. and Folbre, N. (1981) The unhappy marriage of patriarchy and capitalism. In L. Sargent (ed.) *Women and Revolution*. Boston: South End Press.

Farr, W. (1885) *Vital Statistics*. London: Office of the Sanitary Institute.

Firestone, S. (1974) *The Dialectic of Sex*. New York: Morrow.

Foster, R. and Ranum, O. (eds) (1976) *Family and Society: Selections from the Annals*. Baltimore: Johns Hopkins University Press.

Foster, J. (1974) *Class Struggle and the Industrial Revolution: Early Industrial Capitalism in Three English Towns*. London: Weidenfeld & Nicolson.

Gimenez, M. (1980) Feminism, pronatalism and motherhood. *International Journal of Women's Studies* 3(3).

Goody, J., Thirsk, J., and Thompson, E.P. (eds) (1976) *Family and Inheritance: Rural Society in Western Europe, 1200–1800*. Cambridge:

Cambridge University Press.

Grassby, R. (1977) English merchant capitalism in the late seventeenth century: The composition of business fortunes. *Past and Present* 46.

Grieco, M. and Whipp, R. (1984) Women and the workplace: Gender and control in the labour process. Forthcoming in D. Knights (ed.) *Studies of Gender and Technology in the Labour Process*. London: Heinemann.

Habbakuk, H.J. (1940) English landownership: 1680–1740. *Economic History Review* 10.

Hartmann, H. (1979) The unhappy marriage of Marxism and feminism: Towards a more progressive union. *Capital and Class* 8.

Hay, D., Linebaugh, P., Rule, J.G., Thompson, E.P., and Winslow, C. (1975) *Albion's Fatal Tree: Crime and Society in Eighteenth Century England*. New York: Pantheon.

Holt, J.C. (1972) Politics and property in early medieval England. *Past and Present* 57.

Humphries, J. (1977) Class struggle and the persistence of the working class family. *Cambridge Journal of Economics* 1(3).

—— (1981) Protective legislation, the capitalist state and working-class men: The case of the 1842 Mines Regulation Act. *Feminist Review* 7.

—— (1984) The sexual division of labour and social control: An interpretation. Unpublished.

Humphries, J. and Rubery, R. (1984) The reconstitution of the supply side of the labour market: The relative autonomy of social reproduction. *Cambridge Journal of Economics* 8(4).

Hutchins, B.L. (1915) *Women in Modern Industry*. London: G. Bell & Sons.

Kapp, Y. (1972) *Eleanor Marx*. London: Lawrence & Wishart.

Kiernan, V.G. (1976) Private property in history. In J. Goody, J. Thirsk, and E.P. Thompson (eds) *Family and Inheritance: Rural Society in Western Europe, 1200–1800*. Cambridge: Cambridge University Press.

Knodel, J. and Van de Walle, E. (1967) Breastfeeding, fertility and infant mortality: An analysis of some early German data. *Population Studies* 21.

Kuhn, A. and Wolpe, A. (eds) (1978) *Feminism and Materialism: Women and Modes of Production*. London: Routledge & Kegan Paul.

Landes, D. (1975) Bleichroders and Rothschilds: The problem of continuity in the family firm. In C. Rosenberg (ed.) *The Family in History*. Pennsylvania: The University of Pennsylvania Press.

Lane, A. (1976) Women in society: A critique of Friedrich Engels. In B.A. Caroll (ed.) *Liberating Women's History: Theoretical and Critical Essays*. Chicago: University of Illinois Press.

Laslett, P. (1965) *The World We have Lost*. New York: Scribners.

—— (ed., with the assistance of Wall, R.) (1972) *Household and Family in Past Time*. Cambridge: Cambridge University Press.

Laslett, P., Oosterveen, K., and Smith, R. (1980) *Bastardy and its Comparative History*. London: Edward Arnold.

Leffingwell, A. (1892) *Illegitimacy and the Influence of Seasons upon Conduct*. London: Swan Sonnenschein.

Levine, D. (1977) *Family Formation in an Age of Nascent Capitalism*. New York: Academic Press.

—— (1985) Industrialization and the proletarian family in England. *Past and Present* 107.

Marcus, S. (1974) *Engels, Manchester and the Working Class*. New York: Vintage Books.

Marx, K. (1857–58) *Precapitalist Economic Formations*. London: Lawrence & Wishart. (1964 edn.)

Marx, K. and Engels, F. (1845) *Collected Works* vol. 5. London: Lawrence & Wishart. (1976 edn.)

Mathias, P. (1983) *The First Industrial Nation*. London: Methuen.

McLauren, A. (1977) Women's work and regulation of family size: The question of abortion in the nineteenth century. *History Workshop* 4.

Medick, H. (1976) The proto-industrial family economy: The structural function of household and family during the transition from peasant society to industrial capitalism. *Social History* 1.

Meillasoux, C. (1975) *Maidens, Meal and Money (Femmes, Greniers et Capitaux)*. Cambridge: Cambridge University Press. (1981 edn.)

Middleton, C. (1979) Sexual division of labour in feudal England. *New Left Review* 113.

Parent-Duchâtelet, A.J.B. (1836) *De la Prostitution dans la Ville de Paris*. Paris: Chez J.-B. Ballière.

Parliamentary Papers (1840) Appendix to the Sixth Annual Report of the Poor Law Commissioners, Vol. XVII. London: William Clowes for Her Majesty's Stationery Office.

Pinchbeck, I. (1969) *Women Workers and the Industrial Revolution, 1750–1850*. New York: Augustus M. Kelley.

Razzell, P.E. and Wainwright, R.W. (eds) (1973) *The Victorian Working Class: Selections from Letters to the Morning Chronicle*. London: Frank Cass.

Richards, E. (1974) Women in the British economy since about 1700: An interpretation. *History* 59.

Rubery, J. (1978) Structural labour markets, worker organization and low pay. *Cambridge Journal of Economics* 2(1).

Sacks, K. (1975) Engels revisited: Women, the organization of production and private property. In R.R. Reiter (ed.) *Toward an Anthropology of Women*. New York: Monthly Review Press.

Shorter, E. (1971) Illegitimacy, sexual revolution and social change in modern Europe. *Journal of Interdisciplinary History* 2.

Smelser, N.J. (1959) *Social Change in the Industrial Revolution: An Application of Theory to the British Cotton Industry*. Chicago: University of Chicago Press.

Snell, K.D.M. (1981) Agricultural seasonal unemployment, the standard of living and women's work in the south and east, 1690–1860. *Economic History Review* 25.

Springall, M. (1936) *Labouring Life in Norfolk Villages, 1834–1914.* London: Unwin.

Stone, L. (1975) The rise of the nuclear family in early modern England: The patriarchal stage. In C. Rosenberg (ed.) *The Family in History.* Pennsylvania: University of Pennsylvania Press.

—— (1977) *The Family, Sex and Marriage in England: 1500–1800.* London: Harper & Row.

Thompson, E.P. (1976) The grid of inheritance: A comment. In J. Goody, J. Thirsk and E.P. Thompson (eds) *Family and Inheritance: Rural Society in Western Europe, 1200–1800.* Cambridge: Cambridge University Press.

Thompson, E.P. and Yeo, E. (eds) (1973) *The Unknown Mayhew.* Harmondsworth: Penguin.

UNICEF (1983) *The State of the World's Children 1984.* Oxford: Oxford University Press.

Walkowitz, J.R. (1980) *Prostitution and Victorian Society: Women, Class and the State.* Cambridge: Cambridge University Press.

Webb, S. and Webb, B. (1929) *English Poor Law History Part II: The Last Hundred Years.* Private Subscription Edition.

Wilson, S. (1984) The myth of motherhood: The historical view of European childrearing. *Social History* 9(2).

Wray, J.D. (1978) Feeding and survival: Historical and contemporary studies of infant morbidity and mortality. Unpublished background paper prepared for WHO/UNICEF meeting on infant and child feeding, 9–12 October.

3

Marxist and non-Marxist elements in Engels' views on the oppression of women

Martha E. Gimenez

One hundred years after it was first published, Engels' *The Origin of the Family, Private Property and the State* continues to exert its influence upon feminists seeking to establish the determinants of the oppression of women. Whether taken as sources of inspiration or of pitfalls to be avoided, his ideas continue to stimulate theory development and empirical research and have to be confronted by anyone seriously attempting to formulate a Marxist or a neo-Marxist theory of the family and the oppression of women. Engels' views on these topics have been subject to numerous theoretical and empirical critiques; written from different political and academic standpoints, such criticisms have identified weaknesses and ambiguities in his work while recognizing, at the same time, the significance of his achievements.

It is my purpose in this essay to contribute to the debate about the value and meaning of Engels' views by critically examining his major claims in the light of contemporary developments in Marxist and feminist theory. I intend to show that the presence of Marxist and non-Marxist elements in Engels' text is an important determinant of the ambiguous nature of his views. My reading of Engels reflects my background in sociology and my preference for what can be described, for lack of a better term, as a structuralist Marxist perspective.

Engels on the oppression of women

Engels gives us *two* major general theoretical and methodological guidelines for the investigation of the origins of sexual stratification. The first, which is the more abstract, is contained in the controversial, often quoted and often misinterpreted statement in the preface to the first edition of *The Origin*:

> 'According to the materialistic conception, the determining factor in history is, in the final instance, the production and reproduction of immediate life. This, again, is of a twofold character: on the one side, the production of the means of existence, of food, clothing and shelter and the tools necessary for that production; on the other side, the production of human beings themselves, the propagation of the species.' (Engels 1884:71)

Socialist feminists have interpreted this statement in the light of theories that postulate the independent origin of male supremacy. Engels' statement would thus legitimize the separation between the mode of production and the basis of sexual stratification typical of contemporary socialist feminist thought. Socialist feminists acknowledge, however, the role of the organization of production in shaping women's options and emphasize in their writings the need to 'take everything into account'; i.e., the 'mutual interdependence' between 'patriarchy' (or the 'sex-gender system' or 'sexism') and production in general or capitalism in particular (see Sayers 1980:192–97 for an excellent account of socialist feminist interpretations of Engels; and Gimenez 1980:301–10 for a Marxist methodological critique of feminist theory). A more recent and systematic critique of Engels is that of Vogel (1984) who, although critical of socialist feminists' theoretical dualism, reads Engels as they do, thus finding in Engels himself the roots of the 'dual systems perspective' she rejects (Vogel 1984:130).

Engels' second major theoretical and methodological guideline is the following: the oppression of women emerges, historically, with the development of class society. Changes in material conditions making possible the accumulation of surplus wealth lead to the development of social classes and, concomitantly, to the development of the monogamous family, the privatization of household labour, and the transformation of women from respected and acknowledged contributors to communal welfare to domestic servants of their families. This drastic change is institutionalized through the replacement of matrilineal by patrilineal descent ensuring the inheritance of wealth by men's direct heirs: their children. Monogamy and the sexual repression of women to guarantee the legitimacy of heirs are the essence of this change which symbolized, for Engels, the 'world historical defeat of the female sex' (Engels 1884:120).

Is it correct to see Engels as a forerunner of dualistic thinking about the oppression of women? In my view, theoretical perspectives that postulate the independent origin of male supremacy cannot legitimately claim support in Engels' statement nor can they be viewed as an unwitting repetition of 'the failures of the classical socialist tradition' (Vogel 1984:135). They must be understood in their own right, as products of their historical circumstances and a reflection of the limitations inherent in the interpretations of Marxist theory dominant in socialist feminist circles. Ritualistic avoidance of 'economism' and 'biological determinism' tends to lead, unerringly, to dualisms hopelessly mired in the dead ends of multiple causality, multiple interdependence, mutual interaction, and so forth. Last, but not least, another important source of theoretical dualism is the perception, common among socialist feminists, that the status of women in the socialist countries 'demonstrates' that sexism is impervious to changes in the mode of production. As I have argued elsewhere (Gimenez 1980:301–02), such conclusions rest upon an ahistorical, empiricist understanding of the complex question of qualitative social change which, together with the obvious fact that sexism predates capitalism, has lent support to theories postulating its independent origin.

From a Marxist standpoint, Engels' statement is straightforward: it indicates that production has a two-dimensional or twofold nature; that production always entails both the production of the means of subsistence and the production of the producers themselves. The statement reformulates the principles found in *The German Ideology* (1845) according to which the three fundamental premises of human existence are a) the production of material life, b) the constant process through which as needs are satisfied, new needs are created, and c) the production of life through propagation (Marx and Engels 1845:16–17). These three productions are not different historical stages but 'moments' that exist simultaneously (Marx and Engels 1845:17). Dialectically, that is the meaning of Engels' term, 'twofold'. To speak of the twofold nature of production is to refer, at the *metatheoretical* level, to its fundamental moments or aspects. Their mode of articulation in concrete instances, however, varies historically, according to the specific characteristics of different modes of production. Underlying the analytical separation of these dimensions of production there is *the* fundamental premise of historical materialism: 'men must be in a position to live in order to be able to "make history"' (Marx and Engels 1845:16), or, as Engels stated it, 'the determining factor in history is, in the final instance, the production and the reproduction of life' (Engels 1884:71). This premise gives a privileged, *determinant* status to the mode of production although, empirically, the *dominance* of kinship varies according to the characteristics of modes of production and the level of development of their forces of production. In early societies, kinship is the dominant institution and it is impossible to separate it from the 'economy' because kinship relations take on directly the function of relations of production and, as such, they regulate the rights of individuals and groups to the means of production, their participation in production and their access to or share of the total social product (Godelier 1982:285).

Engels did not elaborate, theoretically, on the nature of the relationship between the production of things and the production of life. Instead, he presented a bold and sweeping hypothesis about the origin of the oppression of women which rests upon fundamental changes in the relationship between mode of production and mode of human reproduction: the emergence of the present system of sexual stratification is the result of qualitative changes in production leading to the development of private property, social classes, and the monogamous family. This is a historical and materialistic explanation that does not rest upon the psychological and biological characteristics of individual men and women but on their historical material relations of production and human reproduction. While Engels does take biology into account, it is not biology itself which he identifies as the root of women's subordinate status but the manner in which changes in the mode of production structure the consequences of the fact that maternity, unlike paternity, is never a questionable event (for a thorough discussion of the role of biology in Engels' theory, see Sayers 1982:181–87).

Engels' theory – despite its ethnographic errors – has been considered to be generally correct by some (see, for example, Leacock 1972:7–67; and Sacks 1975:211–34), while others have arrived at more negative conclusions about its worth. For example, Godelier states that, because current developments in the social sciences have proven untenable most of the materials that served as the basis for Marx's and Engels' views on early societies, 'the whole facade of Engels' *The Origin* collapses' (Godelier 1975:103). Vogel (1984) views *The Origin* as a 'defective formulation', a prime example of dualistic thinking because it posits the family as an autonomous category, as the economic unit of society, the social molecule of which society is composed, and opposes to it the realm of industry or public production. This duality is evident, in her view, in Engels' notion of the 'twofold character' of production (Vogel 1984:130).

In the light of these and other criticisms, is it worthwhile to worry about what Engels said or reconsider again, one hundred years after their publication, arguments that would appear to lack substance? My answer to that question is affirmative. His many insights, although never fully elaborated, are important enough to merit reconsideration because they can be used, in conjunction with the theoretical tools of Marxist theory, to further the theoretical investigation of the oppression of women in Marxist terms, thus overcoming the limitations of empiricist and idealist perspectives.

A major source of problems in attempting to interpret Engels' arguments in *The Origin* stems from the fact that Engels did not have a fully developed theoretical framework and proceeds to elaborate his insights in the context of an evolutionary framework alien to historical materialism, 'illustrating' his points about historical stages of change in the family and in the relations between the sexes with numerous examples taken from diverse historical and literary contexts. There is no effort on his part to deal with the issues using the categories of analysis discovered with Marx and developing new ones to grapple with the problems posed by the forgotten dimension of production, the production and reproduction of human life itself. His broad evolutionary theory outlining the changes from pre-class societies, in which kinship is dominant, to 'civilization' (or class society), in which the family is subordinate to the property system, is stated in categories of analysis alien to historical materialism: kinship, women, men, society, family, household labour, monogamy, civilization, etc., are descriptive, not theoretical concepts and, to the extent that *in themselves* they have any theoretical relevance, it lies outside the framework of historical materialism.

For example, it is because he does not formulate the problem of the articulation between the mode of production and the mode of human reproduction in historical materialist terms that he presents an idealist explanation of the emergence of patrilineality and the concomitant 'overthrow of mother right': men's desire to make sure of the legitimacy of their children as heirs to their wealth. Surely, important structural changes in production and in the reproduction of life led to the development of material conditions that made possible not only the emergence of such motives but also their social effectivity; in fact, legitimating accounts of that sort must have appeared *after* fundamental structural changes had led to the overthrow, in actual practice, of matrilineality and its concomitant patterns of male/female relations, division of labour and so forth.

The consequences of the overthrow of mother right are the emergence of the monogamous family, the sexual repression of women, and the privatization of household labour. Lacking a detailed analysis of the twofold character of production in the class-based modes of production that preceded capitalism, Engels describes the effects of the overthrow of mother right upon the family and the relations between the sexes in terms that seem to universalize the features those relations assumed under capitalism at the time Engels wrote. The monogamous family based on private ownership of property, the sexual repression of women, the need for legitimate heirs, the privatization of household labour, etc. are presented as relatively unchanging realities common to all class-based modes of production. In a way, it could be said that there is a latent general theory of class society in Engels' work, class society meaning a form of social and economic and political organization to which correspond exploitative class relations based on the private ownership of the means of production and the private appropriation of the surplus.

This standpoint, which glosses over qualitative differences among pre-capitalist modes of production, has methodological implications similar to those of the sociological perspective, whose object of study is 'society', a totality characterized by a number of universal properties among which 'stratification' or social inequality, and the 'family' are paramount. Engels' own methodological principle as stated in the preface to the first edition should have led him to investigate in detail the articulation between the relations of production in a given pre-capitalist mode of production and their impact upon the relations between the sexes, the conditions for family formation that followed and so forth, thus unravelling the historically specific conditions affecting men and women in different social classes. Instead, he seems to take the two major types of family characteristic of nineteenth-century capitalist society as prototypes to be found in all class societies: the *propertied family*, where marriage is based on economic and/or political calculations, and women are under their husbands' economic and sexual control, and the *propertyless family* presumably based on love and a freely contracted marriage, where the absence of property undermines the authority of husbands while the ability to work and earn wages increases the relative power of wives.

It is obvious that Engels is using nineteenth-century notions about the desirable and undesirable basis for marriage to evaluate marriage throughout history. Monogamy, he argues, is not the fruit of 'individual sex love' but of convenience. Marriage, for all ruling classes throughout history, remains a matter of convenience while among the oppressed classes, marriages based on love are the rule. Marriage, however, is one among the many visible forms that relations of human and social reproduction may take and these relations vary from one mode of production to another. As anthropologists have demonstrated, marriage is not just a matter between individuals but a relationship between larger groups; e.g. households, families, kinship systems, and, depending on the relationship of those larger groups to property, marriages will or will not take place and if they do, it will be under conditions largely independent of the will of the individual men and women concerned. Marriages of convenience reflect the interests of those groups and must be understood in their own right, as the reflection of specific relations of production and of human and social reproduction, rather than as deviations from an idealized marriage based solely on love, or as morally suspect. Because Engels views marriage primarily as a relationship between individuals or, at most, between conniving parents, he fails to elucidate the underlying linkages between class relations and the conditions affecting marriage and family formation in all the social classes that constitute a mode of production at a given point in time. Instead, he focuses on the relations between men and women as such and portrays men as the oppressors and exploiters of women: 'monogamous marriage is the subjection of one sex by the other' (Engels 1884:128); 'the modern individual family is founded on the open or concealed slavery of the wife and modern society is a mass composed of these individual families as its molecules' (Engels 1884:137). While the oppression of women is real, oppression and its forms vary across classes and fractions of classes; and, while some men may benefit from women's domestic services and women's economic and social subordination, male power and the extent to which men may benefit also varies according to class and stratum. This way of posing the problem, as that of one sex oppressing and exploiting the other, is misleading because it transforms the problem of sexual inequality into an ahistorical battle between the sexes.

Elsewhere I have criticized this 'men v. women' problematic which simply examines the relations between men and women at the visible level of social reality or 'level of appearances', as Marx would say. To locate sexual inequality at this level should not be interpreted as an attempt to minimize its importance; it is, instead, the effect of establishing a crucial methodological distinction between levels of analysis. For example, Wright (1978) forcefully stresses the reality of this level stating that people can starve at the level of appearances *even if that starvation is produced through a social dynamic which is not immediately observable.*' (Wright 1978:11; emphasis added). From this methodological standpoint, it can be argued that women are oppressed at the level of appearances; i.e. that the conceptualization of sexual inequality as 'the oppression of women by men' is but a first empiricist approximation to the problem and that its significance in the context of a specific mode of production as well as the identification of the conditions necessary for its emergence, reproduction over time and eventual demise have to be found through the elucidation of its underlying, not readily observable, historically specific determinants. Because he does not investigate the underlying social and economic structures, processes, and contradictions that place *both men and women* in different locations as agents of human and social reproduction, Engels' analysis can reinforce current views on the issue which rest upon non-Marxist theoretical premises or upon idealist and empiricist interpretations of Marxism. These perspectives (e.g. men exchange women; men control women's reproductive ability in their interest; theories of 'patriarchy' in general or of 'capitalist patriarchy'; distinctions between 'private' and 'public patriarchy', etc.) give men a privileged status, as if they alone had had the vision and the power to shape history in their favour, transcending the opacity of social reality and mastering both the intended and unintended consequences of their actions. In the study of sexual inequality, men and women should be viewed as Marx examined social classes. In the preface to the first German edition of *Capital*, Marx wrote:

'I paint the capitalist and the landlord in no sense *couleur de rose.*
But here individuals are dealt with only in so far as they are the
personification of economic categories, embodiments of particular class relations and class interests. *My standpoint . . . can less
than any other make the individual responsible for relations whose
creature he socially remains, however much he may subjectively raise
himself above them.'*   (Marx 1867:10; emphasis added)

Male conspiracy theories of history are just as flawed as class
conspiracy theories. Both men and women are social beings,
'ensembles of social relations', and sexual inequality cannot be
understood in isolation from those underlying, 'invisible' relations,
processes, structures, and contradictions which, at the level of
analysis of social and market relations, pit men and women against
each other.

Another instance of Engels' reliance on descriptive, non–Marxist
categories, is the notion of the family as the 'economic' unit of
society, as the molecule of which society is composed. This is a
typical nineteenth-century sociological truism alien to the Marxist
problematic. Nevertheless, the study of the empirically observable
level of social reality is not outside the purview of historical
materialism; if Engels is to be criticized on this point, it is because
he did not link this 'visible' element of 'society' with its underlying
determinants. It is the case that, at the level of social and market
relations, the family is an economic unit to the extent that it is an
ideologically mystified mechanism that regulates people's access to
the means of production, to the means of subsistence, and to the
goods and services produced in its context by its members. As long
as the family continues to operate as an economic unit, 'society'
does not assume responsibility for its members except under
limited circumstances; distribution and consumption are organized
in ways that presuppose family membership and specific relations
between the family and the 'economy' which severely restrict
women's lives and opportunities.

Under capitalist conditions, the nuclear family, as well as the
other types of households and kinship networks that can be
empirically identified, is the visible structural effect of the

historically specific articulation between the two dimensions of production which determine underlying constraining relations between men and women. The general methodological principle I infer from Engels' analysis is that the material basis of sexual inequality is to be sought in the articulation between class relations or relations of production and the relations of physical and social reproduction valid within a given mode of production. A full theoretical development of the notion that production has a twofold character entails, therefore, the conceptualization of human reproduction in the context of a *mode*; i.e. the historically specific combination of *labour*, and the *material basis* of physical and social reproduction (which includes the *means* – e.g. tools, goods, utensils, raw materials, the household infrastructure – and the *biological conditions* of human reproduction) through the relations of physical and social reproduction, i.e. relations between men and women *mediated* by their relationship to the material conditions of physical and social reproduction. These are relations independent of their will because they are *mediated*, shaped, determined, by their respective relationship to the conditions necessary for their own physical and social reproduction and that of the future generations. At the level of market and social relations, men and women meet as 'free' individuals who bargain with each other on the basis of individual resources such as sexual attractiveness, income, occupation, status, etc. (Collins 1972). Sociologically, those relations are 'free' within severe psychological and structural constraints that reward traditional sex and family roles, marriage, and at least two children as essential components of adult roles, while subjecting those who deviate to a variety of social, economic, and psychological sanctions (Blake 1974). From the standpoint of historical materialism, underlying the realm of 'Freedom, Equality, Property, and Bentham' (and of Romantic Love, Motherhood, The Sanctity of the Home, etc.) are to be found not universal and ahistorical functional, social, psychological, and demographic constraints but historically specific class relations and relations of production which determine the relative access of classes and fractions of classes to the conditions necessary for their physical and social reproduction on a daily and generational level. Just as labour is not the only source of value but *nature* is its necessary material condition, the input of nature cannot be overlooked in understanding the relations between the sexes. Biology mediates; i.e., shapes, modifies the effect of relations of production upon the relations between men and women establishing, just as class relations do, the basis for potentially co-operative and potentially antagonistic relations. The class that controls the means of production also controls the conditions for the physical and social reproduction of the propertyless classes and sets the parameters within which the empirically observable forms of sexual inequality develop and change. This means, consequently, that the mode of production determines the mode of human and social reproduction and that the basis of sexual inequality is not to be found in the intentions and motives of men, either as individuals or as a social stratum, but in the complex interplay between the production of things and the production of human life (see Gimenez 1975, 1980 for a fuller elaboration of these concepts). Engels makes the same point when he states that in the new society (i.e., class society), 'the system of the family is completely dominated by the system of property' (Engels 1884: 72). In his insistence on the importance of the family as the crucial mechanism that supports the oppression of women Engels points the way towards the development of a theory of sexual inequality that surmounts the 'men v. women' problematic and leads, instead, to the investigation of the complex ways in which the mode of production shapes the mode of human and social reproduction and places men and women, as potential agents of production in the twofold sense of the term, in relationships which are a unity of opposites: cooperation and exploitation.

I am aware that the concepts I have presented are very general; they are intended to capture, at the metatheoretical level of analysis, a relationship between the production of things and the production of human life whose historical validity is limited to modes of production based on private property. As historical materialism is not concerned with a general theory of 'class society' but with the study of historically specific modes of production, it is in the context of concrete historical analysis that the theoretical and empirical usefulness of these concepts can be assessed. Given the specific aims of this essay, it would be out of place to include a more detailed presentation of my thinking on these matters.[1]

Although a great deal more could be written about specific problems in *The Origin*, I will end this critical assessment by indicating one last major methodological problem which is manifest in the aim of the book as such: it is a search for *origins*, the origin of the family, private property, and the state, and, by implication, the origin of sexual inequality itself. An important structuralist methodological principle which Marx practised in his work (Godelier 1970) is that which gives priority to structural over historical investigation: 'the study of the internal functioning of a structure must precede and will throw light on the study of its coming into being and subsequent evolution' (Godelier 1970:347).

From this standpoint, what matters is not the chronological order in which features to be found in contemporary social formations have appeared in history but their 'ideal genesis': i.e. their interrelations in the context of a given mode of production and the set of historically specific conditions that created them and reproduce them over time. For example, wage workers are not unique to capitalism; it is possible to find wage labourers under diverse historical conditions. Also, 'capitalists' (i.e. persons using their wealth with the major aim of making profits) have existed in the past. But it would be impossible to understand the uniqueness of capitalism as a mode of production with its own conditions of emergence and its historical laws of motion and transformation if its 'origins' were traced to the earliest historical appearance of propertyless persons working for wages and owners of wealth bent on making profits as merchants or bankers. That would entail the denial of the possibility of qualitative historical change, the transformation of historically specific social classes – capitalists and workers – into ahistorical categories of analysis (e.g. rich and poor or propertied and propertyless) and the universalization of capitalism which, from this ahistorical perspective, becomes either a manifestation of an unchanging human nature or a victory of human reason against the fetters of tradition.

The same argument is valid when the issue under consideration is sexual inequality. A historical materialist approach would not

inquire into the origins of the family or the origins of the
oppression of women in a chronological sense, in prehistory or in
the origins of 'civilization' or class society, but would, instead,
investigate the historically specific structures, processes, and
contradictions characterizing the articulation between the two
aspects of production within a given mode of production. Once
this preliminary task has been completed, three additional necessary tasks remain. First, to establish, theoretically and empirically,
the links between those underlying structures, processes, and
contradictions and their manifestations at the levels of social and
market relations in a given social formation: e.g., segregated labour
markets, sexual stratification, sexual division of labour, dominant
and 'deviant' household structures, etc. Second, to establish,
theoretically and empirically, the links between those underlying,
not immediately observable dimensions of the mode of production
and the dominant ideologies, legal and political structures, and
forms of consciousness. These aspects of social reality which are
not readily observable are the conditions for the effectivity of the
superstructural determinants and manifestations of sexual inequality. Sexual inequality did not originate with capitalism but, from
the standpoint of historical materialism, it cannot be treated as a
survival of earlier times, as a 'historical legacy' (Vogel 1984:153) or
as a phenomenon with an independent origin. The persistence of
sexual inequality has to be understood in terms of the uniquely
capitalist conditions that ensure the *effectivity* of pre-existing
ideologies, forms of consciousness, social practices, etc. Pre-
capitalist forms of sexual inequality may persist and new ones may
emerge and all of them may shape the relations between the sexes
because the capitalist material conditions that place men and
women in unequal relationships determine the *efficacy* of those
patterns.[2] Those patterns have, therefore, an 'ideal genesis' in the
structure and dynamics of the mode of production which have to
be established if the conditions for their persistence and demise are
to be understood. The third important task, once the 'ideal genesis'
of sexual inequality has been outlined, is historical research into the
conditions surrounding the emergence of its elements in a given
mode of production (capitalism, for example) not by tracing their

origins in the transition from pre-class to class society but in the transition, for example, from feudalism to capitalism in Western Europe or to the imposition of capitalism in a colonial or neocolonial context. Engels, however, chose to search for the origins of the family in the origins of class society, an abstraction out of place in Marxist theory. Although Engels never specifically defines it and refers to it as 'civilization', the concept is implicit in numerous statements; for example,

> 'In the collision of the newly developed social classes, the old society founded on kinship groups is broken up. In its place appears a *new society* [emphasis added], with its control centred in the state, the subordinate units of which are no longer kinship associations but local associations; a *society* [emphasis added] in which the family system is completely dominated by the system of property, and in which there now freely develop those class antagonisms and class struggles that have hitherto formed the content of all *written* [Engels' emphasis] history.' (Engels 1884:72)

This family dominated by the system of property is no other than the bourgeois family of nineteenth-century capitalist society which he finds at the threshold of 'civilization' and afterwards throughout history, as depicted in the book. The search for origins always leads to a reading of the past in the language of the present and, in that sense, *The Origin* is no exception. Nevertheless, Engels' awareness and insistence on the crucial determining role of production makes his analysis of the family and the condition of women in 'class societies' infinitely superior to those which postulate the independent and ahistorical origin of sexual inequality.

Conclusion

Besides the problems examined above, other critics have identified additional points of contention. Nevertheless, Engels' work remains extremely important because of those tantalizing glimpses into what a historical materialist analysis of the family and sexual

inequality could be. His insights about the condition of women
under capitalism identify the major structural barriers to real and
substantial changes in the status of women: the privatization of
domestic labour and childcare in the context of the family. His
analysis suggests that sexual inequality is a structural effect of the
articulation between the mode of production and the mode of
human and social reproduction. A qualitative change of the mode
of production leading to the abolition of the family (i.e. the
socialization of domestic labour and of childcare) is the necessary
condition for the development of free and equal relations between
the sexes. It follows, from Engels' premises, that qualitative
changes in sexual stratification are impossible within the capitalist
context. As the experiences of capitalist countries show, the
struggle for women's rights is a long and protracted one in which
victory is always short-lived and limited because the advancement
of individual women – no matter how numerous – is always
predicated upon the oppression of others. While the lot of
working-class women has changed little and women in 'dual
paycheck' families continue to work a 'double shift', upper-middle-
class women in 'dual career families' free themselves from domestic
responsibilities by purchasing the labour of other women. To an
extent likely to vary with income levels and type of occupation, the
'liberation' of some women is predicated upon the existence of a
class of domestic servants, baby sitters, housekeepers, or whatever
other euphemistic names may be used to describe them. From this
standpoint, changes in the division of labour between the sexes (i.e.
greater male participation in domestic work and childcare) which
seem to be 'progressive' and useful for changing sex role
stereotypes, are not only a relatively inefficient form of time use
(hence the preference for purchasing domestic labour in the market
by those who can afford it) but, what is more important, also
contribute to strengthen the family as the major locus for the
reproduction of labour power, daily and generationally.

   It follows also from his premises, that the lack of full equality
between the sexes in the socialist countries (in spite of their
impressive achievements) is itself an important indicator not of the
'failure of socialism to liberate women' but of the extent to which

those societies are yet to experience significant qualitative changes in their mode of production and social organization.

Awareness of theoretical problems in *The Origin* comes easier than the appreciation of its merits and I will end this essay by restating those. In my own experience as a sociologist attempting to establish the material determinants of the oppression of women, I found Engels' frustrating and witty book invaluable as a source of very important methodological insights. My own understanding of these issues has changed since I wrote my first essay on this topic (Gimenez 1975) but I always returned to what I consider to be Engels' major contributions: the concept of the twofold character of production; the centrality of the relationship between system of property and kinship; the economic basis of marriage and the usefulness of understanding family networks as channels for the circulation and distribution of property, goods, and services; and last, but not least, the identification of the structural barriers to equality between the sexes under capitalism and the realization that the material basis of sexual inequality was to be sought at the level of analysis of the mode of production, in the articulation between the relations of production and the relations of physical and social reproduction.

Engels' major achievement is that he forces us to think, in opposition to current ahistorical, universalizing and, for all practical purposes, classless perspectives, *historically and politically* about the question of sexual inequality. Engels sets the basis for a historical analysis, one that rests upon the fundamental premises of historical materialism that posit the ultimately determinant role of the mode of production in setting up the structural boundaries for the relations between men and women, as agents of production and as agents of human and social reproduction. This necessarily entails awareness of the importance of social class, as an element that can potentially bring men and women of the same class together in solidarity while determining irresolvable contradictions between men and between women belonging to opposing classes. This, in turn, not only leads us to question the theoretical and empirical adequacy of characterizing all men as 'the enemy' and all women as 'sisters' but also, and more importantly, enables us to refine the

analysis of women's oppression by examining class and socioeconomic status differences and similarities in the complex and
interrelated dimensions of oppression (i.e. psychological, reproductive, political, social, economic, etc.). Finally, Engels' analysis
establishes a link between sexual equality and qualitative change at
the levels of mode of production and its corresponding social,
political, legal, and ideological structures. Engels may not have
given us all the answers but he has certainly given us some tools to
help us posit the correct questions.

Notes

1. It would not be out of place, however, to examine briefly some
   'visible', empirical structural effects of these underlying determinants in
   order to clarify the meaning of these theoretical propositions. The
   current process of economic transformation in the US leading to the
   relative decline in well-paid manufacturing jobs for men and the
   increase in low-paid 'service' jobs (where there is greater demand for
   women's labour) has profoundly affected the relationship between the
   sexes and the conditions for family formation and stability within the
   working class. The decline in real wages and the demise of the 'family
   wage' have led to the massive incorporation of married women into the
   labour force as a result of economic necessity. Record high unemployment rates have intensified the contradictions of the welfare state and
   this is reflected in the growing number of poor female-headed families,
   particularly among blacks. These and other examples I could give are
   surely well known although they are not usually interpreted as
   empirically observable effects of the ways in which production
   determines reproduction by structuring the opportunities open to
   working-class men and women. Changes in the organization of
   production shape the possible relations between men and women of the
   working class. It should be clear, therefore, that the Marxist standpoint
   according to which the mode of production determines the mode of
   reproduction is not synonymous to 'economic determinism', 'economism' or similar prejudices which reflect, in the current feminist
   literature, a political standpoint rather than a well grounded theoretical
   and empirical critique. It simply indicates that under capitalist conditions, the relations between working-class men and women are
   established within boundaries largely determined, particularly in the
   absence of workers' organized resistance, by decisions taken by those
   who, by controlling the means of production, control the access to the

means and conditions of physical and social reproduction as well. Under capitalist conditions, furthermore, no social class or social stratum is exempt from the determination exerted by the mode of production upon the mode of physical and social reproduction.

2. The fact that feminist ideology does not have a universal appeal to women can help clarify the relationship between material conditions and the effectivity of ideologies. Changes in material conditions (i.e. economic, political, social, and demographic) in the US changed the *actual experiences* of hundreds of thousands of women and led to the development of the women's movement and its corresponding ideologies and theories. Among those generally young, often single or divorced, better educated middle and upper-middle-class women, *the hold of traditional ideologies was undermined because of their changed experiences*. Traditional ideologies lost their efficacy among them because their material conditions had changed, opening to them new opportunities. Likewise, the movement's negative image and the efficacy of traditional ideologies among less educated women of lower socio-economic status or those who see themselves primarily as wives and mothers can be best understood in terms of the material conditions that shape their daily experiences. *Sexist ideologies and practices are dominant in the US* (and in other advanced capitalist countries as well) *because the material conditions that ensure their effectivity have not radically changed.*

References

Blake, J. (1974) Coercive pronatalism and American population policy. In Ellen Peck and Judith Senderowitz (eds) *Pronatalism; The Myth of Mom and Apple Pie*. New York: Thomas Y. Crowell.

Collins, R. (1972) A conflict theory of sexual stratification. In Hans P. Dreitzel (ed.) *Family, Marriage, and the Struggle of the Sexes*. New York: Macmillan.

Engels, F. (1884) *The Origin of the Family, Private Property and the State*. New York: International Publishers. (1972 edn.)

Gimenez, M.E. (1975) Marxism and feminism. *Frontiers – A Journal of Women Studies* 1(1):61–80.

—— (1980) The oppression of women. In Ino Rossi (ed.) *Structural Sociology*. New York: Columbia University Press.

Godelier, M. (1970) System, structure, and contradiction in *Das Kapital*. In Michael Lane (ed.) *Introduction to Structuralism*. New York: Basic Books.

—— (1975) *Perspectives in Marxist Anthropology*. London: Cambridge University Press.

—— (1982) The problem of the 'reproduction' of socioeconomic systems.

In Ino Rossi (ed.) *Structural Sociology*. New York: Columbia University Press.

Leacock, E. (1972) Introduction. In F. Engels (1884) *The Origin of the Family, Private Property and the State*. New York: International Publishers. (1972 edn.)

Marx, K. (1867) *Capital*, vol. 1. New York: International Publishers. (1974 edn.)

Marx, K. and Engels, F. (1845) *The German Ideology*. New York: International Publishers. (1947 edn.)

Sacks, K. (1975) Engels revisited: Women, the organization of production and private property. In Rayna R. Reiter (ed.) *Toward An Anthropology of Women*. New York: Monthly Review Press.

Sayers, J. (1982) *Biological Politics – Feminist and Anti-feminist Perspectives*. London: Tavistock.

Vogel, L. (1984) *Marxism and the Oppression of Women – Toward a Unitary Theory*. New Brunswick, NJ: Rutgers University Press.

Wright, E.O. (1978) *Class, Crisis, and the State*. London: New Left Books.

4

For Engels: Psychoanalytic perspectives

Janet Sayers

> Feuerbach starts out from the fact of religious self-alienation, the duplication of the world into a religious, imaginary world and a real one. His work consists in the dissolution of the religious world into its secular basis. He overlooks the fact that after completing this work, the chief thing still remains to be done. For the fact that the secular foundation detaches itself from itself and establishes itself in the clouds as an independent realm is really only to be explained by the self-cleavage and self-contradict-oriness of this secular basis. . . . Thus, for instance, once the earthly family is discovered to be the secret of the holy family, the former must then itself be criticised in theory and revolutionised in practice.
>
> (Marx 1845:29)

The reason Engels' *The Origin of the Family, Private Property and the State* continues to be so important to feminism is that it draws attention, as does feminism, to the mutability of the family and its sexual divisions. In this, as I shall seek to explain in the first section of this essay, Engels began to fulfil the project set by Marx in his 1845 'Theses on Feuerbach', and continued by him in his notes on Morgan's *Ancient Society*, namely that of spelling out the contradictions that are the source of development and change in 'the earthly family'.

Many feminists have felt that Engels was unduly optimistic in believing that the contradictions wrought by technological advance and by the transition to socialism would fundamentally alter the family, and thereby bring about full equality between the sexes. This has led some to seek to supplement, or even replace Engels' thesis with psychoanalytically-based accounts of the persistence of sexual inequality in the technologically advanced countries of the West and in the socialist countries of the East. I shall consider four such accounts in the second section of this essay.

These accounts, I shall argue, mistake for reality our society's ideology of the family, of 'the holy family', as essentially constant and conflict-free. They thus overlook the contradictions in 'the earthly family' that are the source of this ideology.

This is surprising since it was precisely women's experience of these contradictions that constituted the impetus of the feminism that inspired these theories in the first place. It is even more surprising given the psychoanalytic orientation of these theories. For, as I shall explain in the third section of this article, it was Freud's recognition of the conflicts and contradictions of family life that first led him to develop the theory and practice of psychoanalysis.

Freud made it the business of his clinical work to interpret and thus make conscious such conflicts to his patients. He believed that they would then be able to act to realize their needs and desires. Feminism and Marxism go further. They recognize, as I shall point out in my conclusion, that such realization depends not only on interpreting the world, but also on collective action to change it.

Engels on the contradictions of family life

Engels prefaces *The Origin* with a statement of the dialectical materialist thesis that he intended to inform the whole work. The family, he asserted, is not static and unchanging as it appeared to be to his contemporaries. Instead, he argued, it is in process of constant change and transformation. This, he said, results from the way it comes into contradiction with wider society. 'The social organization under which the people of a particular historical epoch and a particular country live is determined by the stage of development of labour, on the one hand, and of the family on the other' (Engels 1884:71–2). As these forces and relations of production develop, he says, so they come into contradiction with each other and, as a result, 'In the collision of the newly developed social classes, the old society founded on kinship groups is broken up' (Engels 1884:72). Out of this 'collision' are then born new conflicts and contradictions – 'class antagonisms and class struggles'. These in turn lead to still further transformation of society and its sexual divisions.

In the event Engels did not consistently pursue in *The Origin* the dialectical materialist thesis that he had thus announced in its 1884 preface. As feminists have regularly pointed out, he sometimes explained the historical development of the family in idealist and psychological terms (see de Beauvoir 1949; Gimenez this volume), sometimes in evolutionist and biologistic terms (see Kuhn 1978; Maconachie this volume), and sometimes in 'economistic' terms as mechanically rather than dialectically determined by the simple forward march of technological progress (see Vogel 1983; Humphries this volume). On the other hand, he did also seek to explain the history of the family and its sexual divisions dialectically, as the effect of the contradictions arising out of the development of the forces and relations of production. It is this aspect of *The Origin* that I shall detail here.

Engels begins by arguing that it was the development of the forces of production – namely of tools – that brought about the transition from nomadic to settled household living. With the production of bows and arrows, wooden vessels and utensils, plaited baskets, stone tools, dugout canoes, and houses it was no longer necessary or feasible to continue to live nomadically. The development of the means of herding animals and cultivating land also brought forest-dwelling to an end. People now settled in the grassy plains. And as iron tools – such as the axe and spade – came to be developed so the forest came to be cleared with consequent increase and concentration of the population in restricted localities.

At this stage in the development of production, says Engels, 'mother right' obtained in the sense that descent was reckoned through the mother, and in the sense that residence was matrilocal rather than patrilocal. 'The communistic household', he wrote of this stage of the development of labour, was one 'in which most or all of the women belong to one and the same *gens*, while the men come from various *gentes*' (Engels 1884:113). Evidence of this, he said, came from the kinship terminology still in use among the Iroquois of New York State, a terminology that even then was in contradiction with the family relations actually obtaining among this people.

Matrilineal descent, says Engels, came to be overthrown as a result of its coming into conflict with subsequent developments in production. The development of cattle breeding, metal working, weaving, and agriculture, he argues, made it possible to produce an economic surplus in excess of the day-to-day maintenance needs of the communistic household and *gens*. This surplus, he claims, was produced primarily in the men's sphere of activity and its ownership consequently 'fell to the man' (Engels 1884:221). But, under the matrilineal system, descent was reckoned through the mother so that the inheritance of the newly generated economic surplus was also reckoned through the mother's line of descent. It was, says Engels, the contradiction between this development in production and the matrilineal form of the family then in operation that led to the overthrow of this family form, to its replacement by patrilineage in which property was now entailed through the father's rather than through the mother's line of descent. This, he writes, led to the subjugation of women, to their becoming 'a mere instrument for the production of children' (Engels 1884:121).

At the same time, states Engels (1884:142), and especially with the advent of capitalism, property came to be owned on an individual rather than collective basis. And people likewise came to be alienable on an individual basis. The development of the division of labour into 'agriculture and handicrafts' production, he claims, resulted in an intensification of 'production directly for exchange' (Engels 1884:222). And in this process not only commodities, but also women 'acquired an exchange value' (Engels 1884:118). Marriage became an exchange, a contract apparently 'freely entered into by both partners' acting as free individuals (Engels 1884:136) but in fact governed by property and family interest (Engels 1884:142). Out of this development came the possibility of 'modern individual sex love' (Engels 1884:132). He points out, however, that this possibility is not realised within monogamy so long as it is based on economic interest. Until this, the material basis of monogamy, is overthrown, he says, marriage will continue to be either a condition 'of leaden boredom, known as "domestic bliss"' (Engels 1884:134), or one in which husbands and wives only realize themselves sexually through adultery. Either way, the institution of monogamy, itself born out of earlier contradictions between the forces and relations of production, contains within itself new contradictions that in turn undermine it, rendering it no more eternal than the forms of family life that preceded it.

Engels argues that the same economic development – namely the production of economic surplus – which brought into being the institution of bourgeois monogamy that persists into our own times, also brought into being the institution of slavery, and the institutions of feudalism and class exploitation. As 'human labour power obtains the capacity of producing a considerably greater product than is required for the maintenance of the producers' so property-owners came to appropriate to themselves the products of the surplus labour power of the unpropertied classes (Engels 1884:234). Only in the latter classes, argued Engels, could individual sex love be realized, for only here was marriage not contracted on the basis of property interest. (This may explain why, when love fails, unpropertied couples have usually found it easier than propertied couples to dissolve their marriages, at least informally if not formally and legally – see, for example, Stone 1985.) Engels nevertheless acknowledged that marriage in the unpropertied as in the propertied classes is often characterized as much by male brutality as by love. He attributed this to the influence exercised over all classes by the ruling class's ideology of the family (Engels 1884:135) which, as we have seen, involved the exploitation of women in the interests of securing legitimate heirs to men's property.

In his 1845 *The Condition of the Working Class in England*, Engels anticipated that the then contradiction of the forces and relations of production – namely that between the development of factory-based production and its previous domestic organization – would altogether undermine the previous patriarchal organization of the family. Already, he said, the hiring of women and children to work in the factories had made them largely independent of the patriarchal authority of their men folk. In fact, however, women and children never managed to command the same wages as men for their factory work. Indeed this was a major reason why they had been hired to this employment in the first place. The owners of capital have never been willing to provide the facilities – nurseries say – that would enable women and men easily to combine childcare with factory work (Brenner and Ramas 1984). Some have nevertheless contrived to combine these two activities. Of the period when *The Origin* was first published a Mrs Yearn recalls, for instance,

> 'My father was a brick-setter by trade . . . We had the terrible winters of frost and snow, and for six or seven months in the year father was unable to work, so mother had to go to the mill, leaving us in the frail hands of an elder sister. My job was to take the baby into the mill to be fed twice a day.' (Davies 1931:102)

More often, and since childcare continued to fall primarily to them, women did non-factory work that could be more easily combined with childcare, though not without cost to themselves and their children – work such as nursing, midwifery, charring, laundry work, sewing, or taking in lodgers (see e.g. Gardiner 1974). Whatever option they take, married women have regularly found themselves having to work because their husbands' wages are insufficient to cover the upkeep of themselves and their children. (For turn of the century evidence on this point see Lewis 1985.) And this reflects the fact that employers have always sought to minimize the amount they provide for the costs to the worker of maintaining and reproducing himself and his family on a day-to-day basis. Workers by contrast have sought to maximize this provision, as is evident from the struggles by workers in the nineteenth century for an adequate 'family wage' (see e.g. Barrett and McIntosh 1980).

Marx and Engels anticipated that these conflicts of interest between workers and employers, between the propertied and unpropertied classes, would end in socialist revolution, in the abolition of private property, and in the socialization of production. Engels envisaged this involving the full socialization of the services needed by workers for the reproduction of themselves and their families – the socialization of childcare, food preparation, laundry work, and so on. As a consequence of this development taking place, he argued, women would become fully integrated into social production. Sex equality would thereby be achieved. And marriage would then no longer be founded on financial considerations. The way would thereby be cleared for the realization of individual sex love.

In fact, however, the drawing of women into social production, and the increasing socialization of domestic work, or 'private housekeeping' (Engels 1884:139), has not brought about full equality between the sexes as Engels predicted. Many feminists have concluded that sex inequality must therefore be an effect of psychological factors, as well as of the economic factors considered by Engels. And, just as Freudo-Marxists of the 1930s turned to psychoanalysis to explain the persistence of authoritarianism in Hitler's Germany and in Stalin's Russia (Schneider 1976), so too many feminists now look to psychoanalysis to explain the persistence of sex inequality in the capitalist countries of the West and in the socialist countries of the East despite the economic and social changes that have occurred in these countries since *The Origin* was first published. It is to a consideration of the resulting psychoanalytic accounts of sex inequality that I shall now turn.

Psychoanalytic feminism

I shall begin with the account provided by the feminist poet, Adrienne Rich. In her book *Of Woman Born*, Rich returns to the work of the early feminist analyst, Karen Horney, to explain why, contrary to Engels' thesis, socialism has failed to bring about full equality between the sexes. Like Horney, she argues that male dominance in society results from men's attempts thereby to compensate themselves for the envy they feel of the power enjoyed by women in bearing and rearing children. Socialism on its own,

says Rich, is insufficient to bring about an end to men's rule over
women because it does not fundamentally alter the psychological
source of this rule, namely men's envy of women which is bred not
of capitalism but of 'the mother-son and mother-daughter relationship' (Rich 1976:100).

In effect Rich stands Marxism on its head. Marx states: 'It is not
the consciousness of men that determines their being, but, on the
contrary, their social being that determines their consciousness'
(Marx 1859:181). Rich, by contrast, uses Horney's work to argue
that it is not men's and women's social being that determines their
consciousness but that it is their consciousness – men's 'womb
envy' in this case, their envy of women's powers in childbearing
and childrearing – that determines their social being. In this she is
like Bachofen who, according to Engels, argued in his 1861 book,
Mother Right,

'It is not the development of men's actual conditions of life, but
the religious reflection of these conditions inside their heads,
which has brought about the historical changes in the social
position of the sexes in relation to each other.' (Engels
1884:452–53)

Rich assumes the existence of specific 'actual conditions', namely
those of patriarchy, in the very process of seeking to explain them
psychologically, as the product of what goes on 'inside their
[men's] heads'. Why else but for the existence of a male-dominated
social order would men's ideas, their womb envy, take precedence
over women's ideas, their supposed penis envy say, in determining
social relations?

A second psychoanalytically-based account of sex inequality has
been developed by the psychologist Dorothy Dinnerstein (1978).
She looks to the work of another early psychoanalyst – Melanie
Klein – to explain why, despite Engels' predictions to the contrary,
technological advance has not brought about an end to women's
social subordination. Since many readers will be unfamiliar with
Kleinian theory I shall first outline its relevant aspects before
detailing Dinnerstein's use of it.

Klein argues that the infant is endowed from birth with instincts of both love and hate. Since, says Klein, the infant experiences its hatred as disintegrating of itself, it seeks to get rid of it by ejecting it out of itself, by projecting its hatred into its mother. She is then experienced as hating and attacking it. In warding off the 'persecutory' anxiety to which this gives rise, says Klein, the baby seeks to deny its experience of the mother as persecuting, hateful and frustrating. It idealizes her as full of goodness. But this makes it feel depleted by comparison. This gives rise to envy and greed in the baby of the goodness it experiences the mother as possessing at its expense. It accordingly seeks to spoil or empty the mother of the contents of her body. But this leads to new anxieties in the baby lest she retaliate by attacking it in like fashion.

Klein argues that in the normal course of development the instincts of love and hate become integrated. The baby then begins to develop a secure sense of its ego as integrated and whole. It therefore no longer feels the same need to split off its hatred by projecting it into the mother, nor does it feel the same need to split off the frustrating from the gratifying attributes of its mother. It accordingly comes to experience her more realistically as neither all-good, nor all-bad, as a whole person who is both good and bad, loved and hated. But, says Klein, this brings with it 'depressive' anxiety lest in attacking the hated mother it might thereby have lost the loved mother, now recognized to be one and the same as the hated mother. Nevertheless, states Klein, as further ego integration takes place the child begins to feel it has sufficient resources within itself to make 'reparation' to the mother for its past attacks on her. It thereby feels more able to acknowledge the ambivalence of its feelings towards her. And this leads to a still more realistic perception of her and of its relation to her.

Dinnerstein takes issue with this conclusion. She argues that currently children and adults permanently avoid working through the persecutory and depressive anxieties Klein claims to be necessary to their developing a more realistic attitude both toward the sex that first mothers them, and toward themselves, in which they recognize the separateness, independence, and freedom both of the mother and of themselves. Instead of grasping their autonomy and independence as whole, integrated people, Dinnerstein says, children and adults seek to elude their freedom by transferring from dependence on the mother to dependence on rule by men who are not imbued, as are women, with the primordial fears and phantasies of infancy, so little are they involved in infant care.

The solution, says Dinnerstein, to this our current 'sexual malaise' is shared parenting. Children would then no longer be able to avoid working through the persecutory and depressive anxieties involved in realizing their freedom and independence of those that look after them in infancy. Were men to be equally involved with women in childcare, infants would no more welcome domination by men than by women. They would instead seek to be free of rule by either sex and would thus realize themselves as autonomous, independent beings.

In this, however, Dinnerstein ignores, as did Erich Fromm (1941) before her, the material as well as psychological barriers to people realizing the freedom that is supposedly theirs in our society – a freedom that Engels pointed out is more 'legal' and 'formal' than 'real' (Engels 1884:136). Furthermore, Dinnerstein overlooks the evidence that led Klein to conclude that children develop unrealistic phantasies about men just as they do about women. Klein believed that the resolution of these phantasies depends less on the actual behaviour or sex of the people who look after the child in its infancy, than on the child's innate tendency toward integrating the impulses of love and hate with which she believed it to be endowed from birth.

The British object relations school of psychoanalysis takes issue with this, Klein's instinct-based account of child development. Instead it maintains that this development is determined by the mother's handling of the child. This theory has led to the formulation of a third, psychoanalytically-based, feminist account of existing sexual inequalities in society, namely that of the sociologist, Nancy Chodorow (1978).

Object relations theorists, such as the paediatrician and psychoanalyst Donald Winnicott, hold that whether the child develops a realistic sense of its independence and separateness from others, and from the mother in the first place, depends on the mother initially bringing external reality into conformity with the internal reality of the baby's needs. Most mothers, says Winnicott, are 'good enough' in this sense because, just as the baby initially experiences itself as merged with the mother, so too she experiences herself as merged with it. This, he claims, enables her to anticipate the baby's needs before they break up the continuity of its 'going-on-being', which Winnicott took to be the foundation out of which the baby's ego and realistic sense of the world develops.

Chodorow argues that it is in this stage, referred to by Winnicott as that of 'absolute dependence', that the psychological differences she takes to characterize our sexually unequal society originate. Since mothers are opposite in sex from their sons, she says, they do not identify with them as they do with their daughters. Instead they relate to them as separate and different from themselves. Likewise, after an initial period of experiencing himself as psychically merged with the mother, claims Chodorow, the boy relates to her as different from himself. He negates his experience of fusion with her in seeking to forge a separate, masculine gender identity. This identity, says Chodorow, is based not only on negation of the mother but also on positive affirmation by the boy of his identity with men. However, she states, since social production takes men out of the home, this identification is formed on an impersonal and 'positional' basis. Boys identify with men, says Chodorow, not so much through personal interaction with them as through identifying with the roles in which they understand them to be involved. As a result, she maintains, boys grow up well suited to the impersonal and changing role requirements of occupational work, but ill-suited to childcare. By contrast, she claims, girls retain from infancy the sense they then had of mergence with the mother. This is due both to the intensity of their mothers' mergence with them on account of their being the same sex, and to girls having no need to negate this experience in developing a feminine gender identity. As a result, argues Chodorow, girls arrive at adulthood more able than men to merge and identify with their babies' interests in the way object relations theory holds necessary to healthy child development.

In sum: Chodorow argues that our current sexually divided and sexually unequal society, whereby women mother while men work, is reproduced by women's mothering. Like Dinnerstein, she goes on to argue that sex equality will only come about through shared parenting. Only then, she says, will girls and boys grow up with the same capacities for occupational work and childcare.

Her argument has proved extremely appealing to many feminists. Part of its attractiveness lies in the apparent easiness of her solution to sex inequality. Shared parenting seems much more readily attainable than the socialized childcare advocated by Engels. It has accordingly been much canvassed today now that the goal of adequate public childcare provision seems more hopeless of realization than ever. Yet there are also substantial obstacles in the way of achieving shared parenting. Its realization depends on private struggle by women within the home – a struggle that has not been notable in the past for securing significant improvement in their social lot. It also depends on massive reorganization of occupational work so that women earn the same as men, so that it makes as much financial sense for men as for women to take time off work to look after their children. Achievement of the shared parenting advocated by Chodorow also depends, of course, on women having men upon whom they can call to share childcare with them. But this is decreasingly the case as more and more women find themselves bringing up children on their own, such is the increasing number of women only, and women-headed, single-parent households. Chodorow's argument for shared childcare is only compelling so long as one overlooks, as does the object relations version of psychoanalysis on which it is based, the way that childcare and family life generally are structured by external factors (Housman 1982) – something that it was one of Engels' purposes to document in *The Origin*.

Another problem with Chodorow's theory is that it assumes that gender identity is formed on the basis of the child's affirmation or negation of its first female-based identification with its mother. This depends on it recognizing itself to be the same or opposite in sex to the mother. According to Freud, however, this recognition does not occur during the child's first, dyadic relation to the mother. It only occurs later, he says, as a result of the triadic Oedipus complex. This brings me to the fourth and last psychoanalytically-informed feminist theory that I shall consider here – namely that based on the work of the French psychoanalyst, Jacques Lacan.

In her book *Psychoanalysis and Feminism*, Juliet Mitchell sought to use Lacan's 're-reading' of Freud's account of the Oedipus complex to explain the reproduction from one generation to the next of the ideology of the patriarchal family, 'the social history' of which she recognized Engels to have described in *The Origin* (Mitchell 1974:366). Mitchell took issue with Engels' thesis that the exchange of women by men in marriage is confined, as she put it, 'to strictly literate civilization' (Mitchell 1974:369). Instead she argued that patriarchal kinship exchange is universal to all societies – pre-literate and literate alike.

Lacan points out that this exchange is symbolized by the phallus. And, he says, the meaning of this symbol is given, as are all terms in language, by the antithesis of the presence/absence of that which it signifies. The meaning of the phallus, he claims, is first acquired through the Oedipus complex, which Freud claimed to be initiated by the child's recognition in late infancy of sexual difference as involving the antithesis of 'having a male genital and being castrated' (Freud 1923:312). As a result of this recognition, write Lacanian feminists, the child not only acquires the meaning of the phallus signified by this antithesis. It also comes to situate itself as active agent or passive object of the sexual exchanges symbolized by the phallus, as 'exchanger' or 'exchanged' within patriarchal social relations (Rubin 1975:191).

Gayle Rubin (1984) and Juliet Mitchell (1983) are less confident than they once were of the gains to be derived for feminism from Lacan's work. Others, however, remain convinced of its usefulness in this respect (Rose 1983; Alexander 1984). It is to a consideration of this question that I shall now turn, namely whether Lacanian theory or the other post-Freudian theories sketched out above are in fact useful adjuncts for feminism to the account of sexual inequality provided by Engels in *The Origin*.

Psychoanalysis and the contradictions of family life

If Engels presents the family and its sexual divisions as more
mutable than they are in fact, psychoanalytic feminism commits
the opposite error. It presents the family – women's mothering in
the case of the theories of Rich, Dinnerstein, and Chodorow, or
'the paternal function' in the case of Lacanian theory – as
remorselessly reproducing itself and its sexual inequalities essentially unchanged from one generation to the next. It thus arrives at a
basically static account of the family and its sexual inequalities.

This is due to the fact that psychoanalytic feminism largely
neglects the way family life is conditioned by external social
factors, by social production. This neglect has often been justified
in terms of Engels' 1884 Preface to *The Origin*, in which he states

> 'The determining factor in history is, in the final instance, the
> production and reproduction of immediate life. This, again, itself
> is of a twofold character: on the one side, the production of the
> means of existence, of food, clothing and shelter and the tools
> necessary for that production; on the other side, the production
> of human beings themselves, the propagation of the species.'
> (Engels 1884:449)

This, it has been argued, gives the go ahead to feminism to treat
the family and its reproduction separately from social production.
But, as Lise Vogel (1983) and Martha Gimenez (this volume) point
out, this is to overlook the fact that Marx and Engels clearly
regarded reproduction and social production not as independent of
each other, but as aspects of the self-same process, namely that of
production. While reproduction refers to the production by
workers of themselves and their families, social production refers
to the production of goods and services for others apart from their
producers. In fact it was one of Engels' achievements in *The Origin*
to show the division of social from individual production (or
reproduction) not to be historically universal, as psychoanalytic
feminism often presents it as being, but to be specific to a particular
period of history. Social as distinct from individual production
only came about when the forces of production developed to the

point that producers could produce in excess of their own needs and those of their families. Furthermore the distinction of social from individual production is even now dissolving as the services necessary to the latter (those of health, education, and welfare) are becoming increasingly socialized, albeit this advance is being stopped by the cutbacks in public spending now being made by the Thatcher and Reagan governments.

Psychoanalytic feminism not only mistakes for a universal constant the division of individual production (or reproduction) from social production; it also takes the family as we know it to be essentially the same in form and structure across time and place. In this it commits the same error that Engels' contemporaries committed when, as he put it, they took 'the bourgeois family of today' to have been the same for all time as though it 'had really experienced no historical development at all' (Engels 1884:75). Furthermore, in common with those opposed to feminism, psychoanalytic feminism assumes the family to operate in essential harmony with society in reproducing its sexual divisions and inequalities. It only differs from those opposed to feminism in questioning the justice of these divisions. Otherwise, like its opponents, psychoanalytic feminism takes for reality the ideology of the family that holds it to be in basic accord with society in being its fundamental unit, an ideology forcibly expressed by Jerry Falwell of Moral Majority Inc. when he writes 'The family is the fundamental building block and the basic unit of our society, and its continued health is a prerequisite for a healthy and prosperous nation. No nation has ever been stronger than the families within her' (Falwell 1980:121).

It was one of the great merits of Engels' *The Origin* to have demonstrated that this ideology has no universal validity but is instead the product of particular historical circumstances, of the development of private property which he showed to bring into being the family as 'the economic unit of society' (Engels 1884:223).

In assuming this ideology, psychoanalytic feminism overlooks the contradictions that Engels showed to determine it. For it is the business of ideology to conceal such contradictions. It is for this reason that Marx warned against taking the ideology of a society as starting point of investigation into its actual determinants.

> 'Just as our opinion of an individual is not based on what he thinks of himself, so can we not judge of . . . [society] by its own consciousness; on the contrary, this consciousness must be explained rather from the contradictions of material life, from the existing conflict between the social productive forces and the relations of production.'   (Marx 1859:182)

Freud likewise pointed out the inadequacy of 'the data of conscious self-perception' to reveal the contradictions in family and social life that determine 'the profusion and complexity of the mind' (Freud 1940:195). This is because the ego, in Freud's terms, makes it its business to conceal such contradictions from itself.

Engels drew attention to these contradictions in *The Origin* because, unlike psychoanalytic feminism, he premised his enquiry into family life on the evidence of the changes that had occurred and were still occurring in it and its sexual divisions. His inspiration came from outrage at both class and sex oppression. This, of course, was not the inspiration of Freud's work. He was sympathetic neither to Marxism nor to feminism. He arrived at his discovery of the contradictions of family life as a result of his clinical work. Whereas psychoanalytic feminism starts from the apparent smooth functioning of family and society, the starting point of Freud's enquiry was the disruption of social function involved in neurotic symptoms, parapraxes, and jokes. It was his work as a therapist, as I shall now explain, that led him to discover the subjective effects of the contradictions of bourgeois family life – the objective manifestations of which Engels had described in *The Origin*.

It was on the issue of family and sexual conflict that Freud finally broke with his early co-worker, Josef Breuer. Breuer held that neurosis among middle-class women was a product of the monotony of their domestic lot. This however did not explain their resistance to recalling the mental traumas somatically represented in their symptoms. This resistance, argued Freud, could only be explained on the assumption that it is produced by a conflict in the ego over recalling these traumas to consciousness. It was, he said, this conflict that had led to the repression into the unconscious of the memory of these events in the first place. Neurotic symptoms, he argued, are the product of experiences that are felt by the ego to conflict with the proprieties of family life to which it is committed such that it represses them into the unconscious so that they can then only be recalled to consciousness in somatic, not mental form.

He described, for example, the case of a middle-aged widow, one Emmy von N., who suffered from a nervous tic – a clacking noise that interrupted her otherwise coherent speech. The symptom, it seemed, had first emerged on an occasion when she was sitting by her daughter's sickbed and had sought to be particularly quiet so as not to awaken her. The emergence of the noisy symptom on just this occasion indicates, said Freud (1895), that Emmy had then entertained alongside her caring intentions as a mother the contrary intention of making a noise so as to disturb her child. It was the conflict between these two intentions that had rendered the occasion traumatic to Emmy. As a result of this conflict its memory had been repressed from consciousness, the clacking noise being all that remained in consciousness as somatic reminder of its mental content. This symptom had moreover persisted, wrote Freud, because of yet another family-related conflict in Emmy between her sexual desire and her inability to gratify that desire lest in doing so through remarriage she thereby dispossess her daughters of the land and capital wealth that would otherwise be theirs.

In the years following his treatment of Emmy von N., Freud came to regard family conflict as always lying at the heart of neurosis. In particular, he suggested that neurosis is the result of sexual seduction in childhood by a member of one's family, often by a household servant. Freud (1896) arrived at this conclusion by virtue of the fact that his neurotic patients always recalled such incidents in association to their symptoms. Childhood sexual seduction, he argued, only leads to neurosis where the ego is so committed to the conventional proprieties of family life (as essentially asexual) that it represses its contrary experience (of the sexuality of family life) into the unconscious such that this experience only gains conscious expression in somatic rather than mental guise.

Freud soon abandoned his seduction theory of neurosis because treatment in terms of it proved ineffective in relieving neurotics of their symptoms. It seemed that the stories of childhood sexual seduction with which his patients had regaled him were the product of phantasies woven by them in defence against the conflicts they felt as a result of the sexual desires they themselves entertained toward the members of the family who looked after them in infancy. These conflicts, he now argued, are not confined simply to the families of neurotics but occur in all families, neurotic and un-neurotic alike. It was with this discovery – of the universality of infantile sexuality, and of the family conflicts and contradictions involved in it such that their memory is repressed into the unconscious – that psychoanalysis came into being.

Freud (1905b) now came to describe the childhood origins of the capacity for 'individual sex love' – the historical possibility of which Engels had documented in *The Origin*. This capacity, argued Freud, originates in the sensual pleasures the child derives from interacting with members of its family in being fed, cleaned, clothed, and generally looked after by them. It is through these processes whereby the child's day-to-day physical existence is reproduced, said Freud, that the components of individual sex love – those of orality, anality, genitality, and so on – are first brought into being. In time, he claimed, these components become unified and subordinated to genital sexuality. As a result of this develop-ment the child comes to adopt itself, and members of its family, as whole, integrated, individual objects of its sexual desire.

But expression by the child of this, its newfound individual sex love for itself and for members of its family comes into contradiction with society's taboo on autoerotism and incest – a taboo that Freud believed to be first communicated to the child by the way members of its family indicate, explicitly or implicitly, their disapproval of its masturbation and of its expressed sexual desire toward them. As a result of this disapproval, says Freud, the incestuous desires brought into being in the child by the family's physical care of it are repressed into the unconscious.

In the case of middle-class girls, he said, not only is their incestuous desire repressed but so too is all other expression of their sexuality on account of its contradiction with '"civilized" sexual morality' (Freud 1908), a morality that Engels described as that of 'bourgeois monogamy'. Such was the concern of the middle-class families of his time to ensure that their daughters married well, wrote Freud, that they regularly suppressed in their daughters 'any impulse of love . . . which cannot lead to marriage' (Freud 1908:49).

To the extent that this socialization is successful, said Freud, women remain incestuously fixated to the parents by whose authority they thus repress their sexuality. Sexuality is thereby rendered so taboo and abhorrent to them that they often 'turn away from it with unexplained disgust' (Freud 1916–17:399). Freud describes, for example, the case of a young woman who was 'so prudish that she had an intense horror of everything to do with sex and could not contemplate the thought of ever marrying' (Freud 1894:56). She had become virtually agoraphobic so keen was she to avoid any social contact that might arouse her sexual desire.

In other women, said Freud, the family's suppression of their sexuality does not prevent them marrying. It does however render them incapable of enjoying sexual relations with their husbands and this stops them becoming mothers as their socialization had intended. Having been taught to equate sexual enjoyment with that which is forbidden, says Freud, many married women are only able to enjoy sex in adultery, when 'the condition of prohibition is re-established' (Freud 1912:255).

He went on to argue that the woman who is 'too cowardly or too moral to console herself secretly with another man' (Freud 1916–17:430), and who nevertheless remains sexually unsatisfied with her husband, may find gratification of a sort in neurosis, and in over-sexualizing her relationship with her children. But this latter recourse has the effect of prematurely awakening her children's sexuality. And, since this is no more tolerated than is her sexuality, she thereby prepares the way for her children to become neurotic in their turn.

This is a far cry from the account of the family provided by the various psychoanalytically-informed feminist theories considered above. These theories portray the family as in essential harmony with its own and society's interests in the way it inducts children into its sexual divisions and inequalities. Freud recognized that the family does indeed act in accord with society's interests in these respects, that it serves society in bringing up its children, and in teaching them to suppress their anti-social sexual impulses. He pointed out, however, that by this self-same process, the family also acts in contradiction with society's interests in that, by repressing its children's sexuality, it thereby renders its daughters unwilling to marry, or renders them so incapable of sexual satisfaction in marriage that they resort to adultery or neurosis, thereby subverting the very institution of the family that it had been the purpose of their socialization to secure.

Freud's perspective on the bourgeois family is in this respect strikingly similar to that of Engels. Just as Freud insists on the contradictory character of family life, so too did Engels. Like everything else in civilization, Engels wrote, the family is 'double-edged, double-tongued, divided against itself, contradictory' (Engels 1884:130). Whereas Freud drew attention to the subjective effects of these contradictions in making human psychology 'dynamic' rather than static, Engels drew attention to their objective effects in bringing about change in the family and its sexual divisions and inequalities.

Freud was often as scathing as Engels of the bourgeois family. He tells numerous jokes against it, like the following:

'The bridegroom was paying his first visit to the bride's house in the company of the [marriage] broker, and while they were waiting in the salon for the family to appear, the broker drew attention to a cupboard with glass doors in which the finest set of silver plate was exhibited. "There! Look at that! You can see from these things how rich these people are." "But," asked the suspicious young man, "mightn't it be possible that these fine things were only collected for the occasion – that they were borrowed to give an impression of wealth?" "What an idea!" answered the broker protestingly. "Who do you think would lend these people anything?"' (Freud 1905a:103)

Lest the import of this joke against the family be lost on his reader, Freud adds: 'The whole of the ridicule in the anecdote now falls upon . . . the disgracefulness of marriage contracted on such a basis' (Freud 1905a:151). The work of jokes, says Freud, like that of dreams, neurotic symptoms, and parapraxes is to represent the 'embittered criticism and contemptuous contradiction' (Freud 1905a:233) that cannot otherwise be expressed, so at variance is it with our conscious ideals and ideologies about marriage, the family, and social life generally.

Conclusion

It may be objected that, however interesting Engels' and Freud's accounts of the material and psychical consequences of bourgeois monogamy, they are of little concern to feminism today, now that women are so much more free to realize their 'individual sex love' outside the confines of monogamous marriage. In fact, however, such realization is still constrained by economic factors. We still have not reached the situation, anticipated by Engels in *The Origin*, whereby women are no longer obliged 'to give themselves to any man from any other considerations than real love, or to refuse to give themselves to their lover from fear of the economic consequences' (Engels 1884:145).

Women's sexuality is still restricted by economic dependence on their families, husbands, and lovers. This was nicely brought out on a recent Mothering Sunday when, as well as carrying an article extolling the virtues of marriage (Knightley 1985:36), *The Sunday Times* also ran an item on the sufferings of the wife who, deceived by her husband, nevertheless stays with him, tends to his needs, and even irons the shirts he will 'wear to see someone else' (Rogers 1985:39). Perhaps the most glaring example, however, of the way women's lives continue to be circumscribed by the economic constraints of family life is the fact that these constraints force even those who are battered by their husbands and lovers to stay with them lest they otherwise lose their homes and financial security.

Freud felt that his job was done once he had enabled his patients to become fully conscious of such family conflicts, once he had freed them from the fixation of their sexual desire to past family experience. He believed that his patients would then be 'better armed' to deal with the social conflicts of their lives (Freud 1895:393), and hence be able to realize their individual sex love. Engels went further. He recognized that this realization depends on social as well as on individual change, on overthrow of the institutions of private property that presently prevent our fully realizing our needs, sexual and otherwise. It depends on our being freed from the dead hold of the past, of the monogamous inheritance to which the institutions of private property have given rise, so as to be able to realize the possibilities brought into being by this inheritance – those of individual sex love and sex equality. It is because Engels spells this out in *The Origin of the Family, Private Property and the State*, that it remains important to feminism today, a hundred years after its first publication.

References

Alexander, S. (1984) Women, class and sexual differences in the 1980s and 1840s: Some reflections on the writing of a feminist history. *History Workshop Journal* 17:125–49.

Barrett, M. and McIntosh, M. (1980) The 'family wage': Some problems for socialists and feminists. *Capital and Class* 2:51–72.

Brenner, J. and Ramas, M. (1984) Rethinking women's oppression. *New Left Review* 144:37–71.

Chodorow, N. (1978) *The Reproduction of Mothering*. Berkeley: University of California Press.

Davies, M.L. (1931) *Life as We Have Known It*. London: Virago. 1977.

de Beauvoir, S. (1949) *The Second Sex*. Harmondsworth: Penguin. (1972 edn.)

Delmar, R. (1976) Looking again at Engels' *The Origin of the Family, Private Property and the State*. In J. Mitchell and A. Oakley (eds) *The Rights and Wrongs of Women*. Harmondsworth: Penguin.

Dinnerstein, D. (1978) *The Rocking of the Cradle*. London: Souvenir Press.

Engels, F. (1845) *The Condition of the Working-Class in England*. Oxford: Blackwell. (1958 edn.)

—— (1884) *The Origin of the Family, Private Property and the State*. New York: International Publishers. (1972 edn.)

Falwell, J. (1980) *Listen America!* New York: Doubleday.

Freud, S. (1894) The neuro-psychoses of defence. *Standard Edition of the*

Complete Psychological Works of Sigmund Freud S.E. 3. London: Hogarth.

—— (1896) The aetiology of hysteria. *S.E.* 3. London: Hogarth.

—— (1905a) Jokes and their relation to the unconscious. *Penguin Freud Library (P.F.L.)* 6. Harmondsworth: Penguin.

—— (1905b) Three essays on the theory of sexuality. *P.F.L.* 7. Harmondsworth: Penguin.

—— (1908) 'Civilized' sexual morality and modern nervous illness. *P.F.L.* 12. Harmondsworth: Penguin.

—— (1912) On the universal tendency to debasement in the sphere of love. *P.F.L.* 7. Harmondsworth: Penguin.

—— (1916–17) Introductory lectures on psycho-analysis. *P.F.L.* 1. Harmondsworth: Penguin.

—— (1923) The infantile genital organization. *P.F.L.* 7. Harmondsworth: Penguin.

—— (1940) An outline of psycho-analysis. *S.E.* 23. London: Hogarth.

Freud, S. and Breuer, J. (1895) Studies on Hysteria. *P.F.L.* 3. Harmondsworth: Penguin.

Fromm, E. (1941) *Escape from Freedom*. New York: Avon Books. (1965 edn.)

Gardiner, J. (1974) Women's work in the Industrial Revolution. In S. Allen, L. Sanders, and J. Wallis (eds) *Conditions of Illusion*. Leeds: Feminist Books.

Housman, J. (1982) Mothering, the unconscious, and feminism. *Radical America* 16 (6):47–61.

Knightley, P. (1985) Spinster man is a coward. *The Sunday Times* 17 March: 36.

Kuhn, A. (1978) Structures of patriarchy and capital in the family. In A. Kuhn and A. Wolpe (eds) *Feminism and Materialism*. London: Routledge & Kegan Paul.

Lewis, J. (1985) The debate on sex and class. *New Left Review* 149:108–20.

Marx, K. (1845) Theses on Feuerbach. In *Karl Marx and Friedrich Engels: Selected Works*. London: Lawrence & Wishart. (1970 edn.)

—— (1859) Preface to a contribution to the critique of political economy. In *Karl Marx and Friedrich Engels: Selected Works*. London: Lawrence & Wishart. (1970 edn.)

Mitchell, J. (1974) *Psychoanalysis and Feminism*. London: Allen Lane.

—— (1983) Feminine sexuality: Interview – 1982. *m/f* 8:3–16.

Rich, A. (1976) *Of Woman Born*. New York: Bantam.

Rogers, B. (1985) Pull the other one. *The Sunday Times* 17 March: 39.

Rose, J. (1983) Feminine sexuality: Interview –1982. *m/f* 8:3–16.

Rubin, G. (1975) The traffic in women: Notes on the 'political economy' of sex. In R. Reiter (ed.) *Toward an Anthropology of Women*. New York: Monthly Review Press.

—— (1984) Thinking sex: Notes for a radical theory of the politics of sexuality. In C.S. Vance (ed.) *Pleasure and Danger*. London: Routledge & Kegan Paul.

Schneider, M. (1976) *Neurosis and Civilization*. New York: Seabury Press.

Stone, L. (1985) Only women. *New York Review of Books* 32(6):21–2, 27.

Vogel, L. (1983) *Marxism and the Oppression of Women*. London: Pluto Press.

5
Engels: Materialism and morality

Mary Evans

In *The Origin of the Family, Private Property and the State* Engels envisages a world in which the transformation of property relations brings about a transformation in the relations between the sexes. The end of class society, and the entry of women into social production will bring about, Engels argues, a new form of sexual relationships. In a fervour of excitement he writes:

> 'With the transfer of the means of production into common ownership, the single family ceases to be the economic unit of society. Private housekeeping is transformed into a social industry. The care and education of children becomes a public affair; society looks after all children alike, whether they are legitimate or not. This removes all the anxiety about the "consequences" . . . that prevents a girl from giving herself completely to the man she loves. Will not that suffice to bring about the gradual growth of unconstrained sexual intercourse?' (Engels 1884:139)

So in this passage Engels places himself amongst those who see bourgeois society as sexually and socially repressive – indeed, he does more than that, for he proposes a causal connection between bourgeois society and sexual repression which has remained extremely influential to this day. Many later sexual libertarians, including Wilhelm Reich and Herbert Marcuse, were – to a greater or lesser extent – to follow Engels in arguing that the form of property relations essential to bourgeois society forced individuals into limited, and limiting, sexual relationships and marriages.

But the concern of this paper is less with Engels' views on sexuality, than with his assumption that a transformation in the material relationships between the sexes will bring about a moral and emotional transformation. Inevitably this assumption involves a certain model of the social world: one in which personal behaviour is conditioned and structured by material factors. Therefore, a further theme of this essay is the discussion – in the context of the question of relations between the sexes – of the relationship between the material and ideological. Engels' explanation of the subordination of women is unambiguously materialist. I shall argue here that Engels' stress on material conditions, whilst an important element in the explanation of sexual inequality, is frequently reductionist and largely ignores human interventions in the march of history and the construction of the social and emotional conditions of existence. It is true that Marx wrote that 'Men make their own history' but so too, I would argue, do women. Moreover, women – far from being the passive instruments of the needs of class society as they appear in *The Origin* – have frequently articulated, in opposition to the needs both of men and bourgeois society, specific interests of their own. Yet Engels, in his concern to provide a blueprint for the end of the bourgeois family and bourgeois sexual relationships, largely denies the specific interests of women and takes for granted a model of sexual relations based on the interests and assumptions of men. Indeed, one reading of *The Origin* would reveal a subtext which explicitly demands greater male sexual access to women.

One of the central assumptions of *The Origin* is that changes in sexual relations will result from the entry of women into social production in a society in which the means of production have become common property. This belief has now been challenged by feminists: the view that the key to women's emancipation lies solely, or largely, in their economic independence is not one that is accepted by socialist feminists since the evidence from state socialist societies suggests that the entry of women into social production without an accompanying change in the ideology of gender and the social organization of the sexual division of labour institutionalizes the double shift that women work. Society may well 'take care of all children equally' in China or the Soviet Union but neither society extends the state provision of child care that has undoubtedly occurred in these societies to the more radical examination of the domestic and social responsibilities of women and men. Indeed, the exclusion of women from public power is as marked a feature of state socialism as it is of capitalism, and the potential of the socialist state to control sexuality has been amply demonstrated throughout the Eastern bloc countries. There is very little evidence from, for example, either China or the Soviet Union that the state has any interest in encouraging 'that more unrestrained sexual intercourse' which Engels envisages with such enthusiasm. On the contrary, both societies have condemned sexual intercourse outside marriage and labelled homosexuality or erotic expression as bourgeois tendencies. For the sexual libertarian, state socialism as it presently exists is an unsympathetic regime.

It was, however, one of the expressed hopes of Engels that women's entry into social production would transform sexuality and it is apparent that Engels sees bourgeois, class society as repressive as far as the expression of sexuality is concerned. The sexes are forced into 'unnatural' roles and poses by economic pressures: women into false modesty and men into both sexual aggression and sexual infidelity. Indeed, Engels suggests quite explicitly that men are forced into an unnatural, degrading infidelity by the nature of the institution of bourgeois marriage – finding little sexual comfort or consolation in their homes, bourgeois men are 'forced' into adulterous relationships and the accompanying moral compromise. All this, Engels predicts, will change when women have no fear of pregnancy (because of state care for children) or, if they are unmarried, of the social condemnation of illegitimacy, since the distinction between legitimate and illegitimate children will disappear.

We are offered, therefore, a model of future sexual relations which to previous generations of socialists and/or feminists may have seemed attractive. But one hundred years later, and given the lived experience of state socialism, feminism, and a gay movement,

Engels' analysis is deeply problematic. Yet to say this needs justification and explanation. First, it must be said that what is not being questioned here is Engels' condemnation of the forced economic dependence of women on men with its implications for the social control of women and the rigid ordering of sexual relations. But, and it is a very important qualification, it is not supposed here (and hence the disagreement with Engels) that economic independence in itself carries with it the guarantee of the emancipation, be it sexual or social, of women. The problem with Engels' argument is not, therefore, that he is incorrect in identifying the material dependence of women on men as a cause of the inequalities between women and men in capitalism. What is questioned is his stress on this factor as the *sole* reason for the constraints and injustices that he names. Further than this, it must also be remembered that it is specifically in class society that material dependence has the ideological significance that Engels attaches to it: in a society in which production is fully socialized, dependence and independence, at least in the material sense, would have different meanings and certainly not the negative associations that Engels assumed.

This point serves to illustrate a second major problem which I find with Engels: namely his failing to allow that behaviour and thought are structured and organized both by the demands of the material world and the values of the ideological. In one sense, of course, *The Origin* contains a great deal of discussion of ideology, for Engels deals at some length with the history of the construction and articulation of heterosexual love and romance. Distinguishing between what he describes as the 'simple sexual desire, the *eros* of the ancients' and the 'sex love' of nineteenth-century Europe, Engels argues that contemporary western ideas about romantic love are organized around three premises: the potential equality of the sexes in sexual love, the 'intensity' and 'permanency' of sexual love, and finally, a morality about sexual intercourse which stresses, at lest theoretically, the importance of mutual love in sexual relationships. Thus sexual desire is constructed along those lines which we regard in the West as 'normal': that both parties consent to sexual intercourse and that sexual relations take place between people who live, and love, in stable relationships. Sexual desire is not, therefore, simply to be fulfilled at will and at random.

Now it is apparent, from *The Origin*, that it is this model (which Engels accepts is only a model) which Engels endorses: his quarrel with bourgeois society is that it curtails and distorts the fulfilment of this ideal, since neither sex is free from material calculation, in particular the consequences of unwanted pregnancies. Given that this is the case, it is surprising that Engels (unlike Freud) did not identify inadequate contraception as an important contributory factor in women's disinclination for sexual intercourse. But no, contraception – surely a material aspect of gender relations – is not mentioned, and the stress remains on economic constraints. Further than that, the model of sexuality proposed by Engels takes for granted the organization of sexuality as heterosexuality, and a view of sexuality that in many ways is deeply naturalistic for a writer so concerned with exposing the fallacies of 'natural law' arguments. Sexual desire for Engels is, therefore, always heterosexual and premised on two questionable assumptions: the 'gift' of female sexuality to men (Engels speaks of women 'giving themselves' to the men they love) and the inevitability, indeed the naturalness, of male sexual desire for women.

However, in Engels' world of socialized production we have to ask why women would give themselves to men, or indeed enter into social relationships with them at all, except for the specific motive of procreation. When Engels writes that 'Our sex love differs essentially from the simple sexual desire, the *eros*, of the ancients. In the first place, it assumes that the person loved returns the love; to this extent the woman is on an equal footing with the man, whereas in the *eros* of antiquity she was often not even asked' (Engels 1884:140), he implicitly assumed that all the ancients were men. Hence primitive, essential, sexual desire, the *eros* of that great natural world when all the world was young, was located in men, although directed towards women. It was only with civilization that sex love became organized in such a way that women became romantic partners, and partners whose consent to sexual inter-course was necessary to validate the association and distinguish it, socially and materially, from prostitution. But what Engels seems determined to do is to maintain, in a society which has transformed production and abolished private property, a form of sexual relations which is, by Engels' own demonstration, actually derived – for far from entirely acceptable reasons – from that society. Bourgeois society needs heterosexual, individualized love, Engels maintains, in order to maintain and reproduce property relations. Set as he is on abolishing class society, his model of sexual relationships, with its implicit inequality of sexual desire and its highly individualized form of association nevertheless poses the possibility of the maintenance of inequalities, if not of class, then at least of gender. Yet as Engels was to write in the conclusion to *The Origin*, 'Every step forward in production is at the same time a step backward in the position of the oppressed class, that is, of the great majority. Whatever benefits some necessarily injures others; every fresh emancipation of one class is necessarily a new oppression for another class' (Engels 1884:236).

If we were to substitute sex for class in the last sentence we might arrive at an analysis of sexual relations in Engels' post-revolutionary society as one which might, to many feminists, seem more likely, for it is difficult to see how the transformation of sexual relationships which Engels proposes will be as much in the interests of women as of men. Certainly, women will be freed of the constraints of the bourgeois family, and material need, but the sexual emancipation envisaged by Engels seems unlikely to offer the same rewards to women, given that Engels makes some essentialist assumptions about male sexual desire. He writes, therefore, that 'the intense emotion of individual sex love varies very much in duration from one individual to another, especially among men, and if affection definitely comes to an end or is supplanted by a new passionate love, separation is a benefit for both partners as well as for society' (Engels 1884:145). If it was not known that this passage was written by one of the co-founders of historical materialism, it might be supposed that the author belonged to an individualistic tradition which values above all else individual choice and self-expression. My contention, therefore, about Engels' analysis of the position of women in *The Origin* is that it is an analysis which, far from being material, is in fact deeply ideological. A deconstruction of *The Origin* would thus reveal a set of values and assumptions about women which are, in feminist terms, patriarchal.

In using the term patriarchy I am aware, indeed highly conscious, of the problems associated with it. Beechey (1979), Rowbotham (1979), Alexander and Taylor (1979), and others have all discussed the limitations of the term. In using the term here however I use it to describe those values held by Engels which seem to me to be more concerned with the interests of men – as they are constructed in bourgeois patriarchy – than those of women. In particular I would identify the priority which he gives to paid, non-household work and the necessity, indeed the desirability, of male sexual access to women. The lack of interest of classical Marxism in social reproduction, as opposed to social production, has been explored elsewhere, as has the consistent belief in the last one hundred years that heterosexual intercourse is a *sine qua non* of male health and normality. So these two instances of patriarchal thought do not constitute a major theme here: my concern is with the possibility that in adopting materialist analyses of women's oppression socialists have accepted and taken for granted many of the values of patriarchy, in particular the intrinsic value of paid work and the legitimacy – in terms of ascribed social status – of the distinction between the private and the public. Thus the problem for socialist feminists is both with transforming the material conditions of relations between the sexes and challenging ideologies about the sexes that devalue women and women's work. A further objective – and one which I wish to explore here – is that of constructing a morality of and about sexual relationships that is located in the material world.

The issue of morality is one that has barely been considered by Marxists. It is, however, one that should engage the attention of anyone concerned with relations between the sexes, since those relations have, in all societies, been structured and determined by moral codes. Those codes have, as Engels shows, a material basis: for example, adultery, and concepts of sexual fidelity, became important in societies in which the transfer of property is a central preoccupation. But in all societies, whether capitalist or not, sexual behaviour is in some sense regulated by socially accepted and defined norms. It is thus significant that in Engels' non-class society, the society in which private property has disappeared, there will apparently be no social regulation of sexuality: sexual need (organized, as suggested above, on traditional patriarchal lines which assert the dominance and greater power of male sexual need and desire) will be the organizing factor in relationships between men and women. Since production will be socialized, and both sexes freed from the necessity to maintain and be maintained, then those sanctions on the behaviour of men and women which have kept them locked in unions of 'leaden boredom' will disappear.

But what will replace these constraints? And who will determine the nature of the post-revolutionary morality? Both questions have already been raised in practice, and are increasingly being raised in the West as traditional moral codes lose much of their legitimacy. Thus, in the practice of the establishment of socialism in the Soviet Union, in Cuba, and in China, the state attempted, particularly in the years immediately after the socialist revolutions, to develop a socialist morality and abolish a bourgeois moral code. In the case of all three countries what has emerged has been a family and sexual code which is as organized and rigid as anything ever seen in Western capitalism, and largely intolerant of deviations from heterosexual monogamy. The 'leaden boredom' of bourgeois marriage, in the sense of individuals locked in domestic life long after the disappearance of anything approaching romantic love, would appear to be quite easily replicated in socialist societies. Equally, the West – particularly the United States – has seen in the last twenty years a diminution in the authority of the belief that marriage constitutes a contract, and one which entails its members in particular obligations. Barbara Ehrenreich has recently argued that one of the consequences for women of the sexual revolution of the 1960s was the confidence with which men asserted the validity of their sexual needs, at the cost of the interests of their wives and children (Ehrenreich 1983). Comparisons between what might be described as a 'new irresponsibility' and an 'old responsibility' in personal and sexual relations are dangerous, but the evidence of higher divorce rates, the increasing proportion of single parent households headed by women, and the growing disparities in income and life chances between households with and without a male wage-earner all point to a degree of instability in the family life of the West.

Reactions to this phenomenon vary, as do the analyses of its cause. The pro-family Right locates the causes of family 'break-down' in the growing 'emancipation' of women, the 'irresponsibility' of men, and the general decline in moral values that is supposed to have taken place in the years since the Second World War. The Left, generally somewhat confused and embarrassed about the family, locates the causes of family instability in the economic pressures on families, and increasingly – in sections of the Left influenced by feminism – in the central contradictions in the family between the needs of men, women, and children. The Right has never found much difficulty in articulating a family and personal morality of startling clarity and coherence: men should maintain women and children, who in return for this service, should care for men and accept patriarchal authority. It is a view enshrined in law and the institutions of the State. In practice, of course, there is considerable evidence that the reality falls some way short of the ideal, but the point here is that what is being offered as an ideal is coherent and offers at least a measure of reciprocity.

In opposition to this, the Left has found it increasingly difficult to put forward a family, and sexual, morality that does not merely echo that of the Right. The hegemony of the ideal of the family, demonstrated in campaigns for a family wage, in the construction of the Welfare State and in the maintenance, both in Western and state socialist societies, of laws that maintain marriage and procreative sexuality has been a hegemony to which both men and women, of the Right and the Left, have contributed. There have been dissenters from the view that the family in its existing form should be maintained but this tradition of dissent – both libertarian and feminist – has never achieved any wide acceptance in political discourse. The major reason for this, I would argue, and for the strength of conservative – or preservative – values about family and domestic life is that no viable alternative has yet presented itself. The materialist alternative, proposed by Engels, offers little by way of solution to those practical moral questions about the limits of personal responsibility, the conditions in which personal need can be given priority, and the extent of the rights of individuals to assert their own interests, and choices, over those of others. It is, of course, perfectly true that Engels offers suggestions about the conditions in which individuals will make choices about their personal lives, but the determining morality of those choices remains unstated and vague.

One hundred years after Engels, this still remains the case. The Right wishes to enforce the family imperative: men and women must live in monogamous families and accept given determinations of dependence and obligations to maintain. The Left largely subscribes to a worried concern about the family: as Lynne Segal has written:

'The point is that the "ideal family" is no longer typical; it functions as myth. Family ideology needs to change, so that "the family" no longer suggests the married heterosexual couple with children, dependent on a male wage, but instead a variety of possible family forms. . . . Attempts to solve this [problem of the family] by looking back to a supposedly more satisfactory traditional family, where women were both dependent and subordinate, can solve none of our problems today. "Family policies" and trade union demands which recognise and support the variety of ways we now live and care for each other, where men and society generally assume responsibility with women for childcare, domestic life, and the care for all dependent people, could move towards solving many of our "family" problems. This would mean adequate incomes and services, shorter working hours and realistic child benefits, operating in the context of a caring society where men as well as women know the meaning of caring. Then those same family values of love, care and commitment which, if seen as the individual responsibility of women, are oppressive, could extend beyond the confines of gender and home to become an essential part of a society which would liberate us all.' (Segal 1983:23).

The passage is important, and interesting, because it contains the

standard demands of contemporary feminism for changes in family
policies (particularly and most significantly the assumption by the
state and by individual men of a greater share in childcare) and yet
at the same time goes some way to acknowledging our understanding of the term 'family' – an understanding which embraces most
specific relationships with kin and a less clearly defined sense of
responsibility towards certain individuals with whom there is a
sense of community or common cause. There is, therefore, an
acknowledgement that 'the family' is not necessarily a term of
abuse: the mixed possibilities of family, and marriage, first allowed
and suggested by Engels are all reiterated here. Engels' enthusiasm
for the proletarian marriage (so little shared by contemporary
feminists) was an early instance of the way in which the Left has
never entirely condemned the family, only argued for its reorganization. So common ground has always existed between Left and
Right in our culture, and apparently in other cultures as well, that
sexual relationships and above all sexual relationships that result in
the birth of children should be regulated and controlled.

Engels was not, of course, in favour of enforced, life-long
monogamy, or against divorce. He leaves to the individual the
issues of sexual choice and change and gives the state the
responsibility for childcare. Between this blueprint and the model
society suggested by Lynne Segal (1983) there lies therefore another
difference, indeed another ideological presence, in the shape of the
appearance in Segal's argument of the capacity known as 'caring'. It
is interesting that Engels speaks of 'love', Segal speaks of 'care' – a
difference which speaks, then as now, for quite distinct perceptions
by the sexes of the major and central values of human relationships.
The 'facts' of who cares in the family, and the assumptions
underlying these responsibilities, are now being widely discussed
(see for example Finch and Groves 1983).

In speaking of 'love' and 'desire' Engels offers as a motive in
human behaviour a construct that is subject to considerable
ideological and cultural variety: for Engels a major ingredient of
love would appear to be sexual desire. Absent from this understanding of love are, I would suggest, two problems: one, that love
can often be structured by socially created, rather than real, needs,

and second, that there are certain human relationships, for example between parents and children or parents and elderly kin in which love may or may not play a part, but obligations and learned responsibilities are crucial. For these relationships, the expression caring is the more adequate – not least because the word suggests the active ingredient of work in maintaining individual human relationships. It is perhaps no accident that the socialist regimes of the Soviet Union, China, and Cuba have been so wary of Western ideas of romance and romantic love: the romantic loves that burn for the individuals may, for the state, provide nothing except socially disruptive divorce and separation and parentless, or more likely, fatherless children.

These unromantic ideas about individual sex love contrast sharply with the liberation of the passions that was envisaged by Engels (and Havelock Ellis, Wilhelm Reich, Edward Carpenter, and others). Individual liberation is one thing, moral and social regulation quite another. Indeed, regulation of individual sexual relationships is absent from Engels' projections: to quote Marx, 'to each according to his need' will be the organizing principle of the new sexual order. The first problem, as already suggested, is that male needs may be given priority, or given a particular form and structure that inevitably limits certain forms of female choice. The second problem is a wider one that is raised by all discussions for radical social change: how to ensure a new social order that does not substitute one form of repression (or oppression) for another, and how to ensure, in a transformation from capitalism to socialism that the liberties, however bourgeois in origin, are maintained in the new social order. This is not to argue that capitalism allows a greater personal and social diversity than is the case in socialist societies – on the contrary, the capacity of capitalism to eradicate cultures, social differences, and a plurality of patterns of existence is all too obvious in the latter part of the twentieth century. The argument is not, therefore, for the liberality and diversity of capitalism, but it is for the rights and values that have been established and maintained in the face of the hegemony of the values of the market place and the forces of production. Amongst those values are the centrality often given by individuals, particularly women, to the care of individuals and to the importance of the refusal, indeed even the rejection, of the principles of hierarchy, competition, and the public world. In wishing to emancipate women from the household Engels exhibits just that failure of imagination that has constrained so many male socialists – a perception of the household that is formed by an understanding of the bourgeois household, and its inhibiting effects on men.

Yet this perception of the household has clearly been crucially important in the organization of state socialism: in the Soviet Union, China, Cuba, and to a limited extent the European Eastern bloc societies the household, and its needs, have been given an extremely low importance by the party and its bureaucracies. Social production has been all, and if extremely good reasons have sometimes existed for the priority given to the production of certain goods rather than others then it still does not explain the continuing dismissal of household needs and the specific interests of women. Nevertheless, in saying this, the possibility arises that socialist feminists, like male socialists, have been too enthusiastic in their abandonment of specific cultural forms and values in their search for a materialist analysis. An inherent problem for Marxism is that its very 'scientism' and lack of confusing subjectivity leads individuals (and socialist parties) to suppose that once the skeleton of the forces of production has been lain bare, then dressing the new socialist person will present no problems.

But what to wear is a question that is, as at least some people know, a matter of taste, identity, and culture as well as resources. Certainly, the body has to be clothed, but having clothed it at that minimum necessary to maintain life, other, more complex issues arise. So it is with relations between the sexes, and indeed individuals generally. A society needs to guarantee a minimal set of freedoms in sexual relations such as, for example, the freedom from unwanted pregnancies. Some societies do not, as yet, guarantee even that condition of existence, but once they do, other, complex, issues arise. First, questions arise about the nature of a 'wanted' or an 'unwanted' pregnancy. Second, questions surround the assumption of heterosexuality that accompanies contraception, and third, conflicts can develop between an individual's desire for a child and those of both her or his related others and the wider society. The case of the one child policy in China – discussed elsewhere in this collection – raises all these issues: whatever the individual wishes of particular women, it is generally the needs of the society that are given priority. In the case of a society such as China which has only in the last twenty years been able to guarantee a minimal level of subsistence for its population, those social needs would seem to be an essential consideration for any individual. For all that, it is difficult to abandon altogether, in a consideration of social needs, an individual desire for children, or more than one child, or to dismiss the grief of forced abortion.

These questions about children, pregnancy, and the desire of women and men to procreate, all raise issues, and questions, which suggest that a brief discussion labelled 'social reproduction' is barely sufficient. Hence in feminist demands for public child care and shared parenting there lies still a very marked heritage of Engels: a scientific Marxism that meets all social needs with institutional solutions. It is, however, my contention that although the provision of public childcare, paternity leave, and wider support facilities for individuals with young children are all essential ingredients of a restructured socialist society, at least as important is discussion of the values and the motives that inform individual decisions. If state childcare is provided then women can bear children in conditions of greater freedom and security but – and here the case of China demonstrates one problem in this solution – what kind of childcare should the State provide, and if it does, should individuals use it, and if they choose not to, should society accept the loss of their productive/public labour? Equally, in arguing that the State should provide childcare, how should society decide the criteria by which children are socialized? Socialism has generally asserted, at least in theory, the principle that workers should have a considerable voice in the decisions affecting their lives: by the same argument the state might claim – if it takes at least a considerable part in the socialization of children – that it has a legitimate right to establish the values and principles in which children are educated. At present, of course, the state passes on to children certain central norms, but at the same time allows parents certain other 'rights' about their children's education. The confusions created by this situation – what is private, what is not, the boundaries and limits of parents' rights – leads to those notorious cases in which the state does (or does not) explicitly intervene in the lives of children. Writing this in the winter of 1985, it is apparent that at present the British state is only too concerned to make children – particularly the children of miners – directly the responsibility of their fathers: the private, personal responsibility of men for children is being asserted with considerable vehemence.

That this re-emphasis on the duties of individual men for families is being articulated for political reasons is, to socialist feminists, demonstrably apparent. Yet with the Right's assertion of men's responsibility for their children there lies an uneasy note of alliance with feminism, since one of the arguments of feminism has been – both then and now – that men should take a much larger share of the responsibility for their children. In the nineteenth century this concern took the form of the campaigns against the sexual double standard, for a more liberal treatment of 'fatherless' children, and for the more vigorous prosecution of affiliation orders by the courts. Equally, community pressures also demanded that men recognize, and support, their children. This sense of the need for the proper recognition by men of their children is largely absent from Engels, and from many other socialist tracts on the family policy. And the problem of how the responsibility for children should be constructed lies, perhaps, at the heart of the vacillation of socialist regimes between extreme liberalism (the anti-family liberalization of the immediate post-revolutionary years) followed by the reinstitution of rigid pro-family policies as the demands on the state of liberalization become unworkable. Michèle Barrett and Mary McIntosh have most cogently argued the need for changing the world around the family and pointed out that the family can only change – and more importantly develop into a more satisfactory form of association – if other aspects of social life are re-organised. They write:

'We hope that by now it will be clear that we would put nothing in the place of the family. Anything *in its place*, with the world around it unchanged, could probably be little different from the household patterns and ideology that we know as "the family" at present. . . . What is needed is not to build up an alternative to the family – new forms of household that would fulfil all the needs that families are supposed to fulfil today – but to make the family less necessary, by building up all sorts of other ways of meeting people's needs, ways less volatile and inadequate than those based on the assumption that "blood is thicker than water".' (Barrett and McIntosh 1982:158–59)

Yet making the family less necessary is precisely what the majority of socialist societies have not done. On the contrary, many socialist societies (and perhaps China's puritanical state morality provides the best example) have explicitly encouraged the location of sexuality in the monogamous, heterosexual family and done everything possible to maintain a patriarchal nuclear family which differs from that in the West only in the extent to which married women are actively encouraged to enter the labour force. Despite certain movements towards liberalization in the immediate post-revolutionary periods, socialist societies have generally re-verted to traditional forms of family and sexual organization. This reversion provides suggestive evidence that Engels' materialist explanation for the social organization of sexual and family life can be doubly oppressive to women: it encourages socialists to locate the cause of women's oppression solely in property relations and allows socialist states that do transform property relations to remain satisfied that the reorganization of property relationships is sufficient to emancipate women. Engels could therefore be construed as not just wrong, but dangerous, in his analysis, and in his assumption that bourgeois property relations are the major cause of gender inequalities. That is not to say that Marx and Engels are not entirely correct in identifying capitalist property relations as the cause of class inequality, or to deny that women and men both live, in the West, in the context of a society divided by class. But it is to question the validity of assuming that the relationship between class inequality and gender inequality is simple and straightforward.

That the relationship is not simple has now been well established by numerous discussions and debates, and the relationship between patriarchy and capitalism is one of the better documented liaisons of the contemporary world. One point needs to be made about these debates in this context: that it has proved as hard today as in the nineteenth century to integrate into a socialist strategy an acceptance of the particular needs of women that result from their biological capacity to bear children, since the fear of essentialist theories that locate women even more firmly in motherhood and the household remains paramount. But at least as important is a failure to deconstruct the concepts of 'equality' and 'emancipation' that dominate socialist, and socialist feminist, blueprints. Both these concepts involve bringing women into a male, public world – albeit a transformed one. What is not challenged, or changed, is the ideology of equality and emancipation. The problem of bringing individual interests into harmony with those of society was, as Engels quite rightly perceived, a major task for socialism. The issue for socialist feminism is to establish a materialist analysis of women's subordination that – in emphasising class politics – does not follow Engels in assuming that concepts of emancipation, freedom and equality are always similar in their implications for men and women.

References

Alexander, S. and Taylor, B. (1979) In defence of patriarchy. In M. Evans (ed.) *The Woman Question*. London: Fontana.

Barrett, M. and McIntosh, M. (1982) *The Anti-social Family*. London: Verso.

Beechey, V. (1979) On patriarchy. *Feminist Review* 3:66–82.

Ehrenreich, B. (1983) *The Hearts of Men*. London: Pluto Press.

Engels, F. (1884) *The Origin of the Family, Private Property and the State*. New York: International Publishers. (1972 edn.)

Finch, J. and Groves, D. (1983) *A Labour of Love – Women, Work and Caring*. London: Routledge & Kegan Paul.

Rowbotham, S. (1979) The trouble with patriarchy. In M. Evans (ed.) *The Woman Question*. London: Fontana.

Segal, L. (1983) 'The most important thing of all' – rethinking the family: an overview. In L. Segal (ed.) *What Is To Be Done About The Family?* Harmondsworth: Penguin.

6

Engels, sexual divisions, and the family

Moira Maconachie

The Origin of the Family, Private Property and the State has become a common reference point in discussions about the origins of women's subordination. It has a pervasive influence, being popular both within the socialist movement and within the women's movement, if not always for the same reasons. Questioning the origins of women's subordination remains strategically important: we all have assumptions about what past relationships between men and women were like and how they arose. And these assumptions, implicitly or explicitly, influence what kinds of conceptual questions we pose and also influence what kinds of changes we demand in our relationships with men. Also any discussion of the origins of women's subordination has consequences for the women's movement, both in our organizational forms and political practices. For analyses of the origins of women's subordination and its continuity through history affect the means we devise and the choices we make in combating its present forms in our contemporary struggles.

Engels' analysis of the 'world historical defeat of the female sex' (Engels 1884:120) remains contentious both within the women's movement and in relations between the contemporary women's movement and the Left. Feminism has pointed out the dangers of reading any text that purports to analyse the position of women uncritically, and as is often pointed out, Engels is not primarily concerned with providing an analysis of women's subordination.

He is more concerned with giving an account of the emergence of commodity production, class divisions, and the formation of the state, and with outlining a pre-capitalist epoch of political democracy. It is these broader concerns that are generally at issue in discussions of Engels' work with respect to women.

The Origin, part of the socialist canon, is described by Lenin as 'one of the fundamental works of modern socialism, every sentence of which can be accepted with confidence, in the assurance that it has not been said at random but is based on immense historical and political material' (in Aaby 1977:25). Engels' thesis, briefly stated, is that the subordination of women to men occurred simultaneously with the division of society into social classes and the emergence of the state. His book has subsequently and consequently been celebrated on the Left for theoretically demonstrating a necessary link between women's subordination and the rise of private property. It still retains its political importance today for apparently demonstrating links between women's oppression and capitalist exploitation, and therefore for identifying a common purpose for the women's movement with the Left in overthrowing capitalist social relations.

Engels' work is acknowleged within the women's movement more generally, and cautiously, for its emphasis on the social and historical basis of women's subordination, and for providing an early challenge to other more pervasive natural and universal accounts of women's position. His book continues to provide a point of departure for feminists seeking materialist explanations for the subordination of women to men. The purpose of this paper is to examine Engels' thesis on the history of the family and women's place within it. By focusing centrally on his elaboration of the sexual division of labour, I hope to show that Engels retains a naturalistic account of the relations between men and women within the family. It is perhaps worth noting at the outset that in his text Engels never refers to the women's movement of his day, nor does he discuss women's arguments with respect to the family, or the struggles being conducted by women then for equality with men in respect to the law, to education, and to entry into the professions.

The family

During the latter half of the nineteenth century, at the time of Engels' writing, a controversial debate had begun over the role of the family in the history and constitution of society, and over the universality of the patriarchal form of the family. Engels, following Bachofen and Morgan, opposed the predominant view, represented powerfully by Maine, that the patriarchal family form was the earliest form of human society, a natural social grouping, and universally the family form. Arguing for the existence of a prior form of the family to that of the patriarchal family, Engels used evidence collected by Bachofen and Morgan to demonstrate that from a primitive phase of sexual promiscuity a family form arose that was based on the principles of mother-right.

Engels' objective was to present the family as an historically constituted social unit. Within his text he notes

'. . . all our histories have hitherto started from the absurd assumption, which since the 18th century in particular has become inviolable, that the monogamous single family, which is hardly older than civilization, is the core around which society and state have gradually crystallized' (Engels 1884:164)

In his preface to the fourth edition of his book, in 1891, he repeats and emphasises this argument

'Before the beginning of the sixties, one cannot speak of a history of the family. In this field, the science of history was still completely under the influence of the Five Books of Moses. The patriarchal form of the family, which was there described in greater detail than anywhere else, was not only assumed without question to be the oldest form, but it was also identified – minus its polygamy – with the bourgeois family of today, as if the family had really experienced no historical development at all.' (Engels 1884:74–75)

The Origin, first published in 1884, is based on the work of both Bachofen and Morgan. Engels gives credit to Bachofen for seriously documenting the existing evidence of a period of primitive promiscuity, for discovering the existence of mother-right, and for identifying the supremacy of women within the primitive communal household. However, Morgan's work had the greater impact on Engels. Morgan's first book, *Systems of Consanguinity and Affinity of the Human Family* (1871), theoretically outlined a sequence of changing institutional forms of marriage and was based on an analysis of differences between eighty systems of kin terminology. Morgan's assumption, also shared by Engels, was that kin terminology designated either existing or previous biological relationships, and that it was therefore derivative of different historical marriage relations. From his study, Morgan posited the existence of an original state of sexual promiscuity followed by four successive forms of the family, each form demarcated by progressive extensions of the incest taboo to include larger numbers of kin within its ambit. In the consanguine family the only existing taboo was on intercourse between parents and children, the punaluan family then prohibited intercourse between siblings, and the pairing family extended the taboo to prohibit sexual relations between first, second, and third cousins. The final form of the family is the modern monogamous family. This trajectory suggests that progressive limitations have been placed on the number of socially acceptable marriage partners available for any individual member of society.

It is Morgan's second book, *Ancient Society*, published in 1877, that Engels considered the beginning of 'a new epoch in the treatment of primitive history' (Engels 1884:83). In this book Morgan set out to discover reasons for the transition from one institutional form of marriage to another, and concludes that changes in the form of the family are due to the evolutionary development of the 'arts of subsistence' (Leacock 1972:13). He offers a three-stage model of history: from savagery, through barbarism, to civilization, with the corresponding family forms being group marriage, pairing marriage, and monogamous marriage.

Although he was unable to provide an exact fit between developments in the arts of subsistence and changes in marriage

Summary outline of Morgan's schema adopted by Engels

family form	stage of history		arts of subsistence
group marriage	savagery:	lower	fruits and roots
		middle	fish, fire, and meat
		upper	bow and arrow
pairing marriage	barbarism:	lower	cereals, plants, and pottery
		middle	meat and milk from domesticated animals, irrigation for agriculture
		upper	plough and smelting of iron
monogamous marriage	civilization		alphabet and writing

relations and family forms, it is Morgan's endeavour to link changes in the form of the family to changes in subsistence relations that so inspired Engels, for it outlined a history of the family that was, in its intention, materialist.

Engels' general concept of the family is a materialist one. Marriage and family relations are seen to be ways of organizing and ensuring both the productive and the social requirements of the group. Despite his ethnographic errors and inadequacies, and the unilinear evolutionism of his approach, within the context of his own time Engels' work on the history of the family is progressive. The great contribution of Engels and Morgan is that they place the family within social history and make it an object of historical enquiry. And once family relations are subject to historical scrutiny and are no longer seen to be immutable, the forms they assume in society become open to question.

Women's subordination and the division of labour

Engels discusses women's subordination within the context of the family and its changing historical forms. Accepting the idea that the first family form was based on the principles of mother-right and on the dominance of women within the household, Engels goes on to pose the problem of women's subordination centrally in terms of changes in their status within the household. He explains the relative power of women under the system of mother-right as resulting from their superiority within the household, and it is the loss of this superiority, due to economic developments and the overthrow of mother-right, that signals the historical defeat of the female sex. However, because Engels subsumes the question of women's position to that of the family, his account of the defeat of women takes a secondary and subsidiary place in relation to his description of the changes brought about in the family as a result of changes in the division of labour beyond the household.

Engels traces the history of women's subordination back to the transformation of the family into an economic unit within society. This transformation happened, according to Engels, as a result of the development of commodity production, exchange relations, and the accumulation of wealth by men within the family, all of which fundamentally challenged the collective integrity of the gentile constitution:

> 'Under the. gentile constitution, the family was never an organizational unit, and could not be so, for man and wife necessarily belonged to two different gentes. The whole gens was incorporated within the phratry, and the whole phratry within the tribe; but the family belonged half to the gens of the man and half to the gens of the woman' (Engels 1884:164)

During the period of lower barbarism, before the family became an economic unit, the social organization of society is described, by Engels, in the following terms:

> 'The division of labour is purely primitive, between the sexes only. The man fights in the wars, goes hunting and fishing, procures the raw materials of food and the tools necessary for doing so. The woman looks after the house and the preparation of food and clothing, cooks, weaves, sews. They are each master in their own sphere: the man in the forest, the woman in the house. Each is the owner of the instruments which he or she makes and uses: the man of the weapons, the hunting and fishing implements; the woman of the household gear.' (Engels 1884:218)

Engels identifies the existing division of labour between the sexes as 'primitive' and afterwards goes on to discuss the great social divisions of labour occurring outside of the household. He cites the division between hunting and pastoralism as 'the first great social division of labour' and that between agriculture and handicrafts as 'the second great social division of labour' (Engels 1884:220). The appearance of an independent class of merchants marks the third great social division of labour. The accuracy of Engels' account does not concern me here, but his conceptualization of the initial sexual division of labour as 'primitive' rather than 'social', is crucial. This distinction informs his whole approach to the question of women's subordination and his account of the development of capitalism. And it is here that Engels capitulates to naturalistic explanations of the relationship between men and women.

Engels argues that these social divisions of labour not only increased the productivity of labour overall, but that the surpluses generated by these divisions laid the foundations for the development of commodity production, of trade and of the market. However, he critically locates these social changes as occurring outside the family and within what he considers to be the male sphere, under male control and relations of appropriation. He contextualizes women as being within the household, excluded from these changes:

'With the herds and the other new riches, a revolution came over the family. To procure the necessities of life had always been the business of the man, he produced and owned the means of doing so. . . . All the surplus which the acquisition of the necessities of life now yielded fell to the man, the woman shared in its enjoyment, but had no part in its ownership. . . . The division of labour within the family had regulated the division of property between the man and the woman. That division of labour had remained the same, and yet it now turned the previous domestic relation upside down simply because the division of labour outside the family had changed. The same cause which had ensured to the woman her previous supremacy in the house – that her activity was confined to domestic labour – this same cause now ensured the man's supremacy in the house. The domestic labour of the woman no longer counted beside the acquisition of the necessities of life by the man, the latter was everything, the former an unimportant extra. . . . The man now being actually supreme in the house, the last barrier to his absolute supremacy had fallen.' (Engels 1884:220–21)

Women's status alters as a consequence of changes in the division of labour outside the household. Changes in the social division of labour enable men to accumulate sufficient wealth and power to transform relationships within the household: not only are women excluded from the new realm of wealth in society, but women also lose their relative power within the household as well. Within the family men secure their dominance not only economically, but also paternally, as fathers. By subjugating women within the household, men become dominant throughout society. For Engels then, it is the accumulation of wealth by men coupled to the discovery of paternity and the subsequent 'natural' desire by men, as fathers, to secure inheritance relations within the family that ensures the defeat of mother-right and makes women subordinate to and dependent upon men.

In her introduction to *The Origin* Leacock argues that 'in primitive communal society, the distinction did not exist between a public world of men's work and a private world of women's household service' (Leacock 1972:33). Yet Engels' own account of the transition from barbarism to civilization and the consequent subordination of women to men presupposes a division between the spheres of women's work and of men's work. Rather than accounting for the existence of this 'primitive' sexual division of labour, Engels' work presupposes and is based upon it. The assumption of women's responsibility for, and performance of domestic labour, is taken as a given by Engels. He sees this sexual division of labour – men doing the providing and women the domestic tasks – as 'primitive', arising out of the division of the sexes in biological reproduction, and so to inhere in any family form. The idea of a natural procreative family underlies Engels' text, and in this image of the family women are regarded as having a natural and enduring relationship to children and to men: heterosexuality and heterosexual bonding is just taken for granted. Being a woman also automatically entails the responsibility for domestic labour. Even in his proposals for a socialization of domestic labour there is still the assumption that once a social industry, domestic labour will simply take up less of a woman's time and so free her to perform productive work as well. Men are exempted from domestic labour which is prescribed as women's sphere of work 'The emancipation of women will only be possible when women take part in production on a large, social scale, and domestic work no longer claims anything but an insignificant amount of her time' (Engels 1884:221).

The sexual division of labour within the household that allots domestic labour to women is considered to be immutable. Engels poses the problem of the changing status of women in terms of their position within the household because this is regarded as women's natural sphere of labour. Housework is secured as women's work universally and so becomes that unexplored and timeless set of activities performed throughout history by women. Women's labour and contribution is confined to the household until the advent of large scale social production under capitalism.

In sum, the hidden drama with respect to Engels' elaboration of sexual divisions is that women are naturally tied to men, and that women have always performed those domestic duties associated with a household. These domestic tasks and duties are simply referred to by Engels as 'The woman looks after the house, and the preparation of food and clothing, cooks, weaves, sews' (Engels 1884:218). This process of both naturalizing and universalizing the sexual division of labour within the household in terms of women's immutable relationship to domestic labour is further secured by Engels' constant references to the sexual division of labour as that division existing between the family (women's sphere) on the one hand, and social production (men's sphere) on the other hand.

Materialism: The legacy of Engels

This elaboration of the sexual division of labour as a division existing between the family and social production is written into Engels' conceptualization of a materialist analysis of history. Although he identifies the family as a site of production, it is still separated out from social production proper:

> 'According to the materialist conception, the determining factor in history is, in the final instance, the production and reproduction of immediate life. This, again, is of a twofold character: on the one side, the production of the means of existence, of food, clothing and shelter and the tools necessary for that production; on the other side, the production of human beings themselves, the propagation of the species. The social organization under which the people of a particular historical epoch and a particular country live is determined by both kinds of production: by the stage of development of labour on the one hand and of the family on the other.' (Engels 1884:71–72)

This formulation has been hailed by some Marxist and socialist feminists as one of the insights to be gained from a reading of Engels' text. A general opposition of the family to production has been carried over into analyses of domestic labour, and this dualism has also led to an elaboration of multiple distinctions in the use of the concept of reproduction (still understood largely as women's sphere of activity) as opposed to production.

This conceptual dualism which separates the family from social production and which confines women to the sphere of domesticity is not especially useful for feminism, coming as it does from a tradition that views history as determined within one sphere only – the male sphere of production. It is only after he situates women within the household, with domestic labour to perform, that Engels goes on to discuss production proper, that is, the sphere of men's work beyond the household. This is made the site of the great social divisions of labour, and is also the site from which, he argues, all subsequent history is determined. In his view, history and social change are determined beyond the narrow confines of the household. While women are held within the confines of domesticity, the men are 'out there', engaged in the business of historical development and social change: 'The domestic labour of the woman no longer counted beside the acquisition of the necessities of life by the man; the latter was everything, the former an unimportant extra' (Engels 1884:221).

Engels makes the family an object of historical enquiry but regards the relationship between men and women as already constituted. The family unit is an established necessity, and Engels makes this family unit historically subject to changes that occur outside of it and that mould and determine its different forms of existence. Family relations have no dynamic of their own but are determined by external forces: the sphere of production is accorded analytical priority by Engels. The family remains passive before historical development. Almost by sleight of hand, Engels manages to place the family within history but also to confine women within the family, and thereby to displace women from history. It is only once women enter social production, which he argues becomes possible only with the advent of large scale capitalist development, that women enter into history.

The displacement of women

In this final section, I would like to briefly discuss two issues that relate to and also illustrate the displacement of women within the text. The first issue is Engels' confinement of women to domestic labour prior to the development of socialized production processes under capitalism. He argues that women perform the domestic labour while men are, and have always been responsible for procuring the necessities of life. Engels' explanation for the subordination of women is very simple: women's responsibility for, and the confinement of their activities to, domestic labour is the basis of their superior status within the household under the era of mother-right, and it also explains how women came to be excluded from new forms of wealth in society and made subordinate to men. However, his account is challenged by research on women's contribution to subsistence production in precapitalist and noncapitalist societies. This research categorically refutes his premise that 'To procure the necessities of life had always been the business of the man' (Engels 1884:220).

The myth of 'man the hunter' with his dependent woman at the hearth has been unveiled by the recovery of evidence from hunting and gathering, as well as early agricultural communities, showing women to have been major contributors to overall subsistence needs. Slocum, for example, asks 'What were the females doing while the males were out hunting?' and argues that early forms of sociability, coupled with the gathering and storage of food, were undertaken by women for themselves and their children (Slocum 1975:49). Emphasis is being placed on women's participation in social subsistence and contribution to cultural processes, including the development of new implements and methods of production. Women are now recognized as early cultivators who assumed responsibility for providing subsistence not only for themselves and their children, but also for men. Mies further reverses Engels position when she proclaims that 'Female productivity is the precondition for male productivity and of all further world historical development' (Mies 1981:19).

It is impossible to sustain Engels' claim that 'The same cause which had ensured women her previous supremacy in the house – that her activity was confined to domestic labour – this same cause now ensured the man's supremacy in the house' (Engels 1884:221). Those arguments suggesting that the explanation for male domi-nance over women is to be found in the greater significance of the economic role and contribution of men are also untenable. While it is important to challenge the popular pre-eminence given to participation in social production over participation in housework, and the concomitant trivialization of the 'unimportant extra' of domestic labour, we also need to dismiss historical accounts that confine women's participation to the domestic sphere, and thereby deny women's contribution to historical development and social change.

Secondly, I want to consider Engels' critique of contemporary marriage relations and to discuss his evaluation of the impact that participation in social production would have on women's status. Engels contrasts bourgeois marriage relations to working-class associations, and condemns bourgeois marriages for being ruled by capitalist property relations and so becoming simply relationships of financial convenience. Bourgeois marriages, he argues, rest on the institution of prostitution for husbands and the practice of adultery by their wives. His scathing review of the fraudulent monogamy of the bourgeoisie contrasts sharply with his more romantic vision of working-class relationships which, freed from the imperatives of property relations, are able, he argues, to blossom into passionate relationships based on individual sex love

> 'Sex love in the relationship with a woman becomes and can only become the real rule among the oppressed classes, which means today among the proletariat – whether this relation is officially sanctioned or not. But here all the foundations of typical monogamy are cleared away. Here there is no property, for the preservation and inheritance of which monogamy and male supremacy were established, hence there is no incentive to make this male supremacy effective.'   (Engels 1884:135)

Engels' argument is that relationships between men and women among the bourgeoisie are distorted by capitalist economic relations, and that this distortion is the source of women's subordination within marriage and the family. He assures us that with the removal of the considerations of property, 'true sex love' (the return to a 'natural' heterosexuality) will certainly prevail between men and women. It is difficult to conclude that Engels is merely being overoptimistic. These arguments reveal the continuing reductionism at the heart of his thinking about women's position in the family. And again the emancipatory impact of participation in social production is underlined

> 'now that large scale industry has taken the wife out of the home onto the labour market and into the factory, and made her often the breadwinner of the family, no basis for any kind of male supremacy is left in the proletarian household, except perhaps, for something of the brutality toward women that has spread since the introduction of monogamy.' (Engels 1884:135)

Engels states that working women achieve the basis for equality with men once they enter the sphere of social production. This unfortunately assumes that women enter social production on the same footing as men do, and attain equal status and pay. It is the anticipated economic independence and equality for women that is held to transform women's status (brutality aside). But this projection is blind to the existence of sexual divisions within capitalist production itself; these ensure that women perform particular categories of work usually at the lower end of the occupational hierarchies, and so secure the continuing dependence of women upon men as they are so seldom as well paid. The simple dichotomization between the family and production allows women's entry into social production simultaneously to signal their emancipation. That entry into social production has not led to the emancipation of women is true within capitalist societies and is supported by evidence from existing socialist countries as well. Simple productivism has proved a futile strategy. Perhaps where it has had most success is in relegating 'the family' to a position of analytical insignificance. Yet as Emma Goldman reminds us, 'independence, emancipation and equality will continue to be illusory if the narrowness and the lack of freedom in the home is exchanged for the narrowness and lack of freedom of the factory, sweatshop, department store, or office' (in Young *et al* 1981:46).

Conclusion

Questions concerning the 'natural' or 'social' bases of women's subordination to men are raised when reading *The Origin*. The primacy accorded to the economic factors of social production and his account of the sexual division of labour are specifically at issue. Engels' basic explanation for the subordination of women – that their activities were confined to domestic labour – is not supported. Only by naturalizing women's performance of domestic labour is Engels able to conceive of the sexual division of labour as a division existing between the sphere of the family and the sphere of social production. And as a result of this dualism he is unable to pose the problem of sexual divisions as they exist both within the household and generally within the structures and practices of all social production under capitalism. Naturalizing women's domestic relationship to men blinds us to the strategic possibilities of any interchangeability of tasks between men and women, so making current domestic practices appear particularly immutable. While sexual divisions do concern the differential allocation of tasks, they have also involved the elaboration of a network of hierarchical relations that traverse all the social relations and practices of our society. Why these sexual divisions should exist and take the form of power relationships is not posed by Engels. Within the context of this discussion, the dualism and naturalism of Engels' account has left us with a legacy of conceptual difficulties and rigidities.

References

Aaby, P. (1977) Engels and women. *Critique of Anthropology* 3 (9/10):25–53.

Engels, F. (1884) *The Origin of the Family, Private Property and the State.* New York: International Publishers. (1972 edn.)

Leacock, E. (1972) Introduction. In F. Engels (1884) *The Origin of the Family, Private Property and the State.* New York: International Publishers. (1972 edn.)

Mies, M. (1981) *The Social Origins of the Sexual Division of Labour.* The Hague: Institute of Social Studies. (Occasional paper no. 85).

Slocum, S. (1975) Woman the gatherer: Male bias in anthropology. In R. Reiter (ed.) *Toward an Anthropology of Women.* New York: Monthly Review Press, 36–50.

Young, K., Wolkowitz, C., and McCullagh, R. (eds) (1981) *Of Marriage and the Market.* London: C.S.E. Books.

7

Rights in women: Kinship, culture, and materialism

Nanneke Redclift

Engels as forefather

In commemorating the centenary of *The Origin of the Family,
Private Property and the State*, we cannot fail to be struck both by the
continuing relevance of the work as a reference point for a number
of contemporary debates, and by the considerable ambivalence
which marks its author's reputation. The divergence of Engels
from the conceptual project and method of Marx, in whose
memory and in fulfilment of whose aims the work was conceived,
has largely excluded him from serious analysis within Marxist
scholarship. The unilinear, evolutionist concept of history demonstrated in *The Origin* has been seen as a fatally flawed misunder-
standing of Marx's problematic (Levine 1972). Anthropologists,
too, in their reaction against a universal history of social forms,
have tended to be equally dismissive. Thus they have continued to
acknowledge the contribution of Morgan, on whose anthropological work the book was based, despite refuting specific aspects of his
theory. However, they have generally rejected Engels as being of
little theoretical interest (Firth 1984:42). In the final assessment
Engels' importance has frequently been seen as political, rather than
intellectual – his impact that of a committed spokesperson and
inspired popularizer who sacrificed himself for the European

socialist movement, and who had a politically far-reaching influence in excess of his analytic capacity (Levine 1972; Vogel 1983).

It has been left to feminists, both at the time of the first publication of his work and in the more recent socialist feminist re-examination of the concepts of classical Marxism, to provide a reading of Engels in which the distinctive features of his contribution have received fuller consideration. They have acknowledged Engels' foresight in giving the family a central place in social theory, and his recognition, if imperfectly realized, of the significance of sexual relations and the reproduction of labour power. They have been stirred by his visionary understanding of the crucial importance of the transformation of relations between the sexes. They have also turned to him for the basis of a rapprochement between Marxism and feminism. As Coward writes, 'Engels' text deserves detailed consideration for it reveals above all, the political theory by which the woman question became such a problematic area in Marxism while at the same time being absolutely central to it' (Coward 1983:141). Feminist anthropologists have reclaimed his work for its attempt to produce an historically specific account of sexual inequality, to counter the universalistic assumptions about women's subordination that have been prevalent in the discipline (Sacks 1979; Leacock 1972; Rubin 1975).

For them, too, however, the ambiguity of response has been particularly acute. Engels' 'naturalization' of heterosexuality and heterosexual desire, and his characterization of the sexual division of labour as innate rather than socially constructed, is no longer seen as acceptable. The variability of the sexual division of labour across cultures has been well documented in the intervening hundred years, as has the extent of woman's contribution to the food supply in foraging societies, their probable role in the first domestication of plants and animals and in the development of sharing and sociality (Mead 1935; Dahlberg 1981; Zihlman 1981; Tanner 1982). These findings directly contradict some of Engels' fundamental premises. His assumption that the entry of women into social production would provide a sufficient condition for their emancipation has been demolished by the subsequent history of capitalist production. His idealization of the proletarian family serves to underline his bourgeois utopianism. The prioritization of the sphere of production in *The Origin*, and his failure to carry through the implications of the famous passage on the mutual determinacy of production and reproduction, while seen as a source of his strength for some (Sacks 1979), is regarded as a crucial weakness by others (Rubin 1975). For many it confirms his inability to confront the significance of ideological practices, and prevents him from seeing reproduction in anything but procreative terms. It is also evidence of the underlying conceptual dualism of his analysis, again at odds with Marx. This dualism enables the category of 'family' to be considered as autonomous, rather than rooted in the process of social reproduction as a whole (Vogel 1983). Furthermore, the analytic priority he gives the role of the family in mediating the connection between private property and the State, prevented the realization of any real examination of divisions between the sexes. In assuming this mediating role, it also became subservient to the crucial political issue of the relation between property and the State, rather than being itself the intrinsic object of concern (Vogel 1983).

These comments by no means exhaust the empirical and theoretical responses to *The Origin*, which themselves reflect a conflicting set of political and intellectual priorities. Whether one is ultimately a supporter or a detractor depends not only on these priorities, but also on the presuppositions of the various disciplines from which Engels has been viewed. The relative weight accorded to the hindsight of subsequent research has also produced divergent assessments. Thus feminists have championed him for his enlightenment in the context of the nineteenth century, or denigrated him for the androcentrism which the feminist paradigm has revealed.

The twentieth century retreat from speculative universal laws into the detailed description, classification and analysis of specific societies has also led to a wholesale rejection of his problematic. A result of this, as I shall show, is that certain relevant questions have dropped from view. Conversely, where these questions have been salvaged it has often been with an uncritical reading of other aspects of his work. To some extent this has to do with the partisan nature of acceptance and rejection. Rarely has any other nineteenth-century thinker been so simultaneously appropriated and pilloried. A comparison with the volume on kinship studies produced for the centenary of the publication of Morgan's *Systems of Consanguinity and Affinity in the Human Family* is revealing. 'Today (Morgan's) fame is secure' wrote Fred Eggan in the Introduction. He proceeded to define his task as one of tempering the praise that had been lavished on Morgan since the thirties and which had culminated in the dedication of Lévi-Strauss' *The Elementary Structures of Kinship* to 'the pioneer of the research method modestly adopted in this book'. Further examples of the esteem in which Morgan was held had been provided by Fortes' *Kinship and the Social Order: The legacy of Lewis Henry Morgan* (1969) and Terray's glowing exposition of Morgan's materialism in *Marxism and 'Primitive' Societies* (1972). Thus, although the particular sequences adopted by Morgan for the development of kinship systems have long been abandoned (Eggan 1972), and the study of 'kinship' itself as a unitary phenomenon has been largely rejected (Needham 1971), Eggan concludes 'that he went astray is less important than that he provided us with a series of problems which have occupied our attention for the past century'. British anthropologists have always perhaps been more reserved in their assessment of Morgan than the American school, and have reacted more forcefully against comparative generalization, in favour of the detailed ethnography of individual societies. Nonetheless, whether because of anthropology's greater conservatism, reverence for the ancestors, or simply the sheer mass of empirical work that was generated in the succeeding hundred years, the rejection of Morgan's theoretical framework has left his position largely unassailed.

One reason for this is to be found in the greater influence that Morgan's *Systems*, rather than his monumental *Ancient Society* (Engels' main source) has had on anthropology. The more specialized terms of reference of the former, and the fact that its object – kinship – came almost to be the defining characteristic of the discipline, so that discussion has frequently centred on the identity of the discipline itself, is one factor that seems to have ensured its continuing importance. Thus, to reject Morgan could be seen as tantamount to rejecting the labour of a century of disciples.

In contrast to this Engels' attempt to link productive relations, property relations, the rise of the State, and forms of the family in one vast conceptual scheme was at once more audacious and much more suspect. For many anthropologists the confusions and contradictions this gives rise to in the book itself condemn it to incomprehensibility. Aiming to be both analysis and political programme, the work risked being unsatisfactory on both counts, and having something to say to historians, political economists, sociologists, and feminists, it is hardly surprising that it has been attacked by all.

At this stage there is perhaps little to be gained from entering the debate on these terms. This has been more than adequately done by others elsewhere and in this volume. Rather than examining the work of Engels *per se*, I therefore use it as a starting point for a general assessment of the debate that followed, stimulated and also constrained by many of the assumptions to be found in *The Origin*. The anthropological aspects of the book are frequently avoided as *terra incognita* by feminists from other disciplinary backgrounds, who modestly disclaim their competence in judging 'the anthropology' and confine their discussion to the implications of the latter parts of the book. But the parts are not really detachable from the whole, and the fact that the 'anthropological' issues have been developed in a separate and specialized debate has been detrimental to both sides. It has, in some feminist work, led to the generalization of features of the nineteenth- and twentieth-century Western European family and, more seriously, to an uncritical acceptance of the reification of 'the family' as a valid entity.

This is not only an academic issue, but important for feminist politics, where the assumption that the nature of family is similar for all women, has been one of the divisive issues in international feminism. In anthropology, it has contributed to the creation of a highly specialized research domain called 'kinship' in which gender is absent as a theoretical issue, or reduced to a mere placing mechanism in the service of something else.

Not only has this inhibited the analysis of sexual divisions, as Coward argues (Coward 1983), but it has deflected attention from an understanding of the way that gender relations are embodied as kinship relations; or from an examination, in the light of the ethnographic evidence we now have, of the ways in which forms of kinship and forms of sexual oppression may be linked.[1] This has been largely confined to the critique of the exchange of women as a defining feature of culture as propounded by Lévi-Strauss, the analysis of matrilineal societies, and the recent discussion of the work of Meillasoux. The subsequent separation of the anthropological discussion of kinship and the feminist discussion of the family has been limiting to both. It has been in part responsible, both for the excessive sterility of formalistic studies of kinship terminologies, and for the reification of women as the objects of kinship logic (Aaby 1977) so that geneological space has come to have the abstract properties of linguistic structure.

Gayle Rubin's imaginative essay (1975) argued that, despite their own inability to see the implications of what they wrote, a feminist reading of Engels, Lévi-Strauss, and Freud could provide conceptual tools for developing a theory of the 'sex-gender system' that could have a cross-cultural validity but still remain culturally and historically specific. She suggested that the notion of a sex-gender system was useful because it presupposed nothing about the actual content of the arrangements through which any society transforms biological sexuality and procreation into a set of relationships, assumptions, gender identities, needs, and desires. Rubin put forward this concept because she regarded the concept of 'reproduction' as an inadequate explanation of the diversity of human sexual arrangements that anthropology had revealed. All human groups 'need' to reproduce themselves, but these needs are transformed in ways that are never 'natural', or even always successful; or which are sometimes successful at the expense of the reproduction of other groups, societies, clans, strata, or classes. The relations of reproduction themselves are embodied in a variety of different cultural forms of kinship. Nor could the needs of reproduction of labour *explain* 'the incredible array of Byzantine fetishized indignities' to which women had been subjected (Rubin

1975). For her, the sex-gender system included, but was more than, sexuality or reproduction in the biological sense (see Rubin 1984 for a development of her views).

As Rubin pointed out, Engels' implication that relations of sexuality could be distinguished from relations of production and have a certain autonomy had never been 'followed up and subjected to the refinement it needs'. Opinions differ as to Engels' real position with regard to this autonomy. It is also a fundamental area of disagreement in subsequent feminist work. His starting point, and hers, was the theory of kinship systems which, among many other things, consist of and reproduce forms of socially organized sexuality. For Engels it was important to incorporate kinship into the materialist hypothesis, despite its incongruity, because it enabled him to situate historically the monogamous family that was to be the focus of his critique. I argue that one of the reasons why his project has not been built upon or effectively criticized is because of the divergence between the 'woman question' and the study of sexual inequality on the one hand, and the study of kinship by anthropologists on the other. This is partly attributable to the positions that have been taken in response to the work of Engels or Morgan.

In this paper, then, my aim, rather than to assess Engels, is to assess the debate which succeeded him. To do this I discuss three of the intellectual lineages that derive from the forefathers: kinship studies, Marxist anthropology, and feminism. It is a deliberately selective view, which makes no claims to be a general account of what has been produced in each area, but which examines how certain questions have come to be formulated and others excluded.

The ties that bind: Kin, blood, and gender

The relationship between the biological events of conception and procreation, the perceptual frameworks through which these are understood, and the socioeconomic organization of individuals and groups, has been at the centre of the battleground between the social sciences during the century. By looking at the development of the discussion of kinship within anthropology we can see why an exploration of the material basis of kinship in its relations to forms of sexual inequality has not been pursued.

For Morgan, kinship classification, the nature of the terminology used to refer to 'the community of blood' (Morgan 1871:10), reflected actual biological relations and depended on the marriage form, which he defined as 'the ties that arise out of the biological facts of human reproduction'.

> 'Kinship was about the way in which a people grouped and classified themselves as compared with the real, true, biological facts of consanguinity and affinity. The facts of consanguinity mean those persons who are related by biological descent from the same ancestor. The facts of affinity are the facts of marriage, and marriage means the sexual reproduction relationship between male and female.' (Schneider 1972:34)

Thus kinship terminology was a direct expression of genetics and biology, and from it was derived the form of classification adopted by each society. Terminologies were not random but systematic and could be compared with each other and classified into broad types. Modes of classification provided the clue to the kinds of relationship that a given society established and recognized as significant. Like geological strata they might persist even as practices began to change. For this reason they offered an insight into the past and a chance to capture the movement and change of unrecorded preliterate societies.

These assumptions were initially marshalled in the service of history. For lacking statistical data about the 'real' world of such societies, terminological patterns seemed to offer a way into some of the questions of nineteenth-century speculative sociology. They were amenable to collection as 'data', and their regularity and systematic nature appeared to offer a precision parallel to the analysis of the natural world, a way of reducing the chaos of human experience to the structural elegance of science. Kinship classification was at once empirical and abstract, detailed and generalizable. Morgan's work was thus a source for the comparative method, a method continually disputed yet always central in social anthropology. It can also be seen as the precursor of the rule-bound nature of subsequent kinship analysis, and for the attention given to different varieties of model building, mathematical, grammatical, or otherwise.

Since the nineteenth century the nature of these kinship 'facts' has been repeatedly questioned. An emphasis on the social meanings of kin ties has taken precedence over biological relationships, which have often been found to be unknown, erroneous, or simply irrelevant to the 'real' purpose of such ties (Schneider 1972). Thus 'kin' often turned out to have little to do with 'blood', but to define a number of other characteristics, such as 'those with whom we share rights in land' (Carroll 1968; Leach 1961), or 'those we assume as members of our group'. As early as the 1930s Mead had shown that for the Arapesh the father of a child was the man who had fed her, regardless of biological parentage, and increasing evidence was collected to show that beliefs about the process of conception often de-emphasised the role of the individual genetic pair. Kinship thus came to be seen as providing a metaphysical expression through which to organize groups of people, express economic or political alliances, or solidify significant relationships based on other criteria, casting doubt on 'whether kinship terms are really as wedded to genealogy as we think our own are' (Carroll 1968).

Fortes, for example, who emphasizes the biological aspect of kinship writes 'All Tale genealogical connections go back to the fact of procreation' (Fortes 1949:135) and 'Two "facts of life" necessarily provide the basis of every family: the fact of sexual intercourse is institutionalized in marriage, the fact of parturition is institutionalized in parenthood' (Fortes 1959:149).

Yet, in spite of his acknowledgement of the symbolic and psychosocial dimensions he is mainly concerned with 'kinship in relation to the social structure' (Fortes 1949). Kinship is seen as a means of organizing social activities and relationships. Fortes is more interested in the generational and developmental cycle by which groups are formed and reformed than in the content of the bonds that are created.

By the early 1970s these transformations of kinship were themselves being called into question, reflecting the uncertainties that had hovered around the subject for the previous three decades (Malinowski 1930). In England, Needham argued that 'the current theoretical position is obscure and confused' (Needham 1971:2), and suggested that 'Kinship is certainly a thoroughly misleading term and a false criterion in the comparison of social facts. It does not denote a discriminable class of phenomena or a distinct type of theory' (Needham 1971:cviii).

He argued against attempts at the formulation of general propositions and the emulation of 'natural science', and restricted himself to adopting

'the minimal premise that kinship has to do with the allocation of rights and their transmission from one generation to the next. These rights are not of any specific kind but are exceedingly various: they include most prominently rights of group membership, succession to office, inheritance of property, locality of residence, type of occupation . . . *they have no connection with the facts, or the ultrual idioms, of procreation.*' (Needham 1971:3–4; emphasis added)

Significantly, he goes on to say,

'It is true that the possession and exercise of these rights is defined by reference to the sex of the persons thus related; but then so is the division of labour in the simpler societies, *yet we do not for that reason think this method of distinguishing statuses so remarkable as to deserve a special designation or to call for a distinct type of theory.*

'These jural systems and their component statuses can be genealogically defined. Why this should be so is a fundamental question that has never been properly resolved and I cannot take it up here . . . the label [kinship] designated no distinct type of phenomena; it provides no clue to comprehension. . . . To put it very bluntly, then, there is no such thing as kinship and it follows that there can be no such thing as kinship theory.' (Needham 1971:5; emphasis added)

Since we do now recognize that a theory of the sexual division of labour is called for, we may also feel that the rest of the passage needs some reconsideration. Here it is enough to underline another striking feature of the perspective outlined which is that the basic problem with which it is concerned is methodological/ epistemological rather than substantive. The notion of rights, contracts, and statuses predominates, but because the main point of the argument is to deny that there can be any universal definition, there can also be no room for discussion of the content of these relationships. A final paradox is that Needham's dismissal of kinship as a special kind of phenomenon is organized into sections based precisely on those special categories of which it is conventionally supposed to be comprised, i.e. descent, marriage, terminology, and incest.

A similar problem was faced by Schneider, whose much quoted article 'What is kinship all about?' was published a year later. His approach resembles Needham's in some respects, but also differs in important ways. He, too, argues that there is no such thing as kinship, it is a non-subject. 'It is a theoretical notion in the mind of the anthropologist which has no discernable cultural referent in fact.' (Schneider 1972)

He goes on to qualify this statement in much the same way as Needham, and to stress that what is wrong is actually the process of universalization, the process of studying kinship as if it were 'a distinct, discrete, isolable subsystem of every and any culture'; instead one must escape from the analyst's arbitrarily defined domains into the categories which the culture defines as its parts, through the 'symbolic definition and designation' of that culture.

Again it is clear that the emphasis is on epistemology and the problems posed by the comparative method. But although Schneider restricts his own 'minimal definition' to the specific context of the American kinship system, and criticizes the 'followers of Morgan' (citing Goodenough, Lounsbury, Rivers, Durkheim, Leach, Needham, and Lévi-Strauss), for a social definition whose ultimate referent is still biological, his own position in fact appears to be much more 'biological' than that of Needham. Its basic idea is that of

'shared bio-genetic substance and diffuse enduring solidarity.

. . . The biological elements have symbolic significance. They
constitute an integrated set of symbols in the sense that they are a
model for how life, in certain of its aspects, is constituted and
should be lived. The symbols are "biological" in the sense that
the culturally given definition of the symbol system is, that it is
derived from the facts of biology as a process of nature itself. But
it is fundamental to our understanding that we appreciate that
these biological elements are symbols and that their symbolic
referents are not biology as a natural process at all' (Schneider
1972:45)

Both these accounts, which should be seen as indicative rather
than representative of a very broad field, take the intellectual
history of British social anthropology since the 1920s, with its
emphasis on the interrelation of social institutions within specific
cultures, and push it to its logical conclusion. Both agree that it is
not enough to argue, as some of their predecessors had done, that
kinship is a flexible metaphor for a number of other relationships,
rather than the expression of biological reality. The category itself
as a comparative tool is suspect. Malinowski had pointed out as
early as 1926 that we could only talk of families, not *the* family. For
Needham, all that is possible is the 'resolution of particular
problems and the analysis of individual systems'. For Schneider,
the social systemic approach of the followers of Morgan is replaced
by his belief that kinship functions to answer cultural problems
about meaning and the maintenance of particular patterns of
solidarity. He argues further that the kinship system is broader than
kin classification implies, and that an accurate account of kinship
classification cannot be given without taking the whole system into
consideration. Thus, it is a myth that kinship terms are a guide to
the kinship system. We need to know what is the *domain* of kinship
for each culture, whereas the categories inherited from Morgan and
used by his followers, 'derive from social system questions,
functional questions and evolutionary considerations, all of which
are quite foreign to any particular culture'. They therefore 'protect'
their users from finding out what the 'true units of kinship in a
cultural sense are'.

It might equally be argued that this apparent obsession with the reality and comparability of the 'units' of kinship, has provided us with a distinctly curious answer to the question 'what is kinship all about?' This answer appears to have more to do with the construction of anthropology as a discipline, than with an examination of what this metaphorical transformation of the biological is and does; why it constructs, explains, signifies, in a particular way. Without at this stage prejudging what an adequate answer to such a question might be, or even that it is answerable in such a form, we can at least note some of the elements that are absent from such a perspective.

The anthropology of kinship provides us with a wealth of evidence about the organization of sexual relationships, but little which questions the basis on which these relationships are produced. Either sexual relations take second place to other organizational principles or they are seen as simply one aspect of an integrated whole, structured through kinship as an institution. Sexuality is potentially disruptive; 'kinship' brings system and order, norm, and rule. We come to know a lot about sex but little about sexual divisions or the construction of gendered subjects through the relations of reproduction. Any idea that sexuality or sexual divisions are a relevant, or problematic, aspect of kinship is missing from these accounts. In essence the attack on biological theories inevitably led to the repudiation of such an analysis. Thus biology is often referred to in a gender neutral way or both it and 'human reproduction', with which it is often conflated, are rejected or subordinated to other concerns. This deconstruction of kinship and its reconceptualization 'as economy', 'as politics', 'as language' etc., certainly demonstrated the mutability of biology. However, it did more than that. It suggested that sexual relationships lay in the biological domain and were therefore basically irrelevant to a sociological understanding of the function of kinship.

Thus, in the work of the twentieth-century inheritors of Morgan, a process of exclusion and subsumption takes place: kinship is about this and not that, it is generational continuity rather than physical bonds, it is meaning rather than reproduction, it is reproduction rather than . . . We have no way of telling whether or not this might be merely a reflection of the societies under study; but we *can* say from the theoretical assumptions followed that many of the questions we would want to raise today cannot be asked. As Barnes remarks in *Three Styles in the Study of Kinship*, his comparison of Murdock, Fortes, and Lévi-Strauss,

> 'Our writers assume that we have under scrutiny the orderly actions of homogenous societies, where norm and mean are closely in accord. Even if with Lévi-Strauss we concentrate our attention on thought rather than action, we are still dealing with homogeneous thinking without serious cleavages of thought based on wealth or power.' (Barnes 1971:265)

There is little in these reassessments to enlighten us as to the nature of relationships between men and women, in terms of power, dominance or equality. Little to suggest that anthropology can contribute to the study of theories of reproduction or the perception and regulation of sexuality. To say this is not to reject the things that kinship has been said to *be* or *do* or necessarily to invalidate the organizational and symbolic dimensions that have been revealed, but merely to note the process through which both the biological question (even in its social form) and the issue of gender equality raised by Engels has become inadmissable.

Kinship and unconscious representation

When feminists have looked to anthropology for development of some of the questions first suggested in *The Origin*, it is to the work of Lévi-Strauss that they have turned, although his relationship to the Marxist tradition is ambivalent. Why has Lévi-Strauss' theory of kinship been so influential despite the critical reactions that it has provoked? And, more importantly for the purposes of the argument presented here, in what ways does Lévi-Strauss' idiosyncratic interpretation of the concerns inherited from the nineteenth century contribute to our understanding of the intersection of kinship and gender?

The anthropological perspective we have discussed so far begins with the question 'How does society work?' Gender is implicit in this analysis, but it occupies a descriptive place, concealed by the theoretical problems of the comparative method. The question posed by Lévi-Strauss is, rather, 'How does man conceive of himself in relation to the world of society?' We note his assumption that *male* self-conceptions exhaust all possibilities in the formation of identity. Nevertheless, Lévi-Strauss' insistence on the search for unconscious categories, and on the cultural representations produced through kinship systems, appears to offer the promise of a bridge between the psychoanalytic account of the subordination of women via the construction of sexuality in the family, and the culturally specific forms which these relationships assume. Kinship is predicated on difference, and difference is *the* problematic for feminism. As we have seen, kinship studies since Engels have frequently assumed this as given, and taken as their object the insertion of kinship into the totality of social relations. Lévi-Strauss' elaboration of the analogy between kinship and language, in focusing on differentiation and classification as the intrinsic cultural act, also suggests that some of the blank spaces we have identified in other texts might be filled (Coward 1983). In some places, too, he seems to capture the essence of contradiction and ambivalence that has also been lacking.

Thus the social world is

> 'that to which social life ceaselessly bends itself, in a never wholly successful attempt to construct and reconstruct an approximate image of that world of reciprocity which the laws of kinship and marriage, in their own sphere of interest, laboriously derive from relationships which are otherwise condemned to remain either sterile or immoderate.' (Lévi-Strauss 1969:490)

The appeal of this idealist notion of social relations for some feminists (who have tended to extract what they see as the spirit of the piece rather than being too concerned with precision of meaning, or lack of it) has been that it seems to recognize desire and the structuring of sexual relations through particular signifying systems and practices ('the laws of kinship'), which are expressed in systems of exchange and substitution ('that world of reciprocity'). As Fleming argues in her defence of Lévi-Strauss, 'By means of this a precarious representation of the world is constructed and reconstructed, and by the same means representations can be challenged and subverted' (Fleming 1983:24).

His account differs from the symbolic approach exemplified by Schneider, as well as from the materialism of Morgan and Engels, in his assumption that the significant object is culture itself, as an elaboration of the human mind, rather than the expressive modalities of individual cultures. This, too, promises to offer an insight into questions about the necessity of patriarchy and the universality of women's subordination with which feminists have been concerned.

However, there are many ambiguities in the text, and to base a feminist defence on the tension of imperfect symbolic resolution, or as Rubin does on the fact that *The Elementary Structures of Kinship* is 'permeated with an awareness of the importance of sexuality in human society' (1975) is to read or extract a meaning that seems largely external to it.

Like Engels, Lévi-Strauss takes for granted many of the things that require an explanation. It is difficult to do justice to the complexities and internal inconsistencies of his work as a whole here, but a few passages can be selected as indicative: 'The emergence of symbolic thought must have required that women, like words, should be things that were exchanged' (Lévi-Strauss 1969:496) and 'The relationship of reciprocity which is the basis of marriage is not established between men and women, but between men by means of women, who are merely the occasion of their relationship . . . the woman is never anything more than the symbol of her lineage' (Lévi-Strauss 1969:116) and 'The first logical end of the incest prohibition is "to freeze" women within the family so that their distribution, or the competition for them is within the group, or under a group not private control' (Lévi-Strauss 1966:21).

Even where Lévi-Strauss retreats a little from the negation of 'merely', the reduction to nothingness, and the definition of women in terms outside themselves, as 'the object of personal desire', 'the subject of the desire of others', it is at best a grudging retreat. 'But woman could never become just a sign and nothing more, since even in a man's world she is still a person, and since in so far as she is defined as a sign, she must be recognized as a generator of signs'. (Lévi-Strauss 1969:496).

Since his inspiration, too, is Morgan rather than Engels and his object not history and empirical reality, but models, which cannot be reduced to actual relations, it has been argued that he is dealing in abstractions and is not concerned with concrete relations between men and women at all. Thus there is no theoretical reason why it should be women who are the objects of exchange. From this perspective, the linguistic analogy, which compares kinship to a communication system, is 'neutral' and cannot presuppose anything about the subordination of women. The notion of the exchange of women by men in a cycle of reciprocity which links groups together through time and space, providing basic and indissolvable human bonds presupposes nothing about power and domination, just as the structure of language tells us nothing about the relations between the users of it. From this point of view, actual practice is not at issue. For example, in testing the theory against the empirical evidence of one African society, Singer maintains, 'it is not a woman that is being replaced or renewed, but a social network' (Singer 1973). Lévi-Strauss himself, in a passage of uncharacteristic self-exoneration, explains 'The female reader . . . can easily find comfort in the assurance that the rules of the game would remain unchanged should it be decided to consider the man as being exchanged between women's groups. . . . Some *very few* societies of a highly developed matrilineal type have attempted to express things that way' (Lévi-Strauss 1956:284).

Is it therefore only in matrilineal societies that the rules can be reversed? If so, the comfort is meagre since such societies represent only approximately 15 per cent of the world's cultures (Murdock 1957; Gough 1961:663). Moreover, to draw the implication that males could theoretically be substituted for females in any context is totally at variance with other statements made by Lévi-Strauss that women are 'the valuables *par excellence*' (1969:481) and that it is a 'basic fact that men exchange women and not vice versa' (1969:115).

I shall come back to the issue of the implications of matrilineality for women. It seems clear, however, that Lévi-Strauss's model is not theoretically neutral. The sex of exchangers and exchanged, sign and signifier, is entailed by other conditions, and based on a set of premises that feminists would want to question; and if this supposed neutrality *could* be regarded as an accurate reading, then the model would simply be 'gender-blind' and it could equally be argued that it had little to offer.

As Barnes puts it, 'It is easy to think of these groups of men which interchange women living, as it were, on some air-conditioned Olympus. They marry and give in marriage, but that is all. They toil not neither do they spin and their need for shelter for the night is not apparent' (Barnes 1971). Questions about subjectivity, consciousness, economics, are simply outside the terms of reference of the model and inadmissable. Nor are any suggestions offered as to the consequences and outcomes of unconscious representations, or the deep structures of exchange implied by the argument. The differences between the systems considered have no implications for real-world experience.

In fact the purity of this abstraction is flawed in some places. One is that Lévi-Strauss frequently refers to 'control' as well as to 'exchange' of women. More seriously he does provide an 'explanation' of *why* women are the objects rather than the transactors in the creation of bonds of reciprocal exchange. This is because of their special 'value' and scarcity, which makes them naturally desirable by naturally promiscuous men. This, as Coward points out, directly contradicts Saussurian premises in which language is simply a system of differences without pregiven meaning. The assignment of value must therefore be logically secondary and inscribed within the meaning system of specific cultures (Coward 1983). It is true, then, that sexuality is fundamental to the model, but in an entirely contradictory way. At one level everything about it is prejudged; at another, the paring down of kinship to communication prevents the control of sexuality and reproduction being seen as in need of explanation.

Emanuel Terray (1972) has defended Morgan from the empirical criticisms levelled at him, by saying that it was not his aim to write a history of humanity, but to construct a *theory* of that history, in other words 'a system of concepts to make it possible to think it out scientifically'. Similarly, Lévi-Strauss has resisted the devastating attack on the empirical inaccuracies of his ethnography (Korn 1973), and his misreading of the data of others, by purporting to offer a theory of culture as superstructure. Thus cultural variation in actual sexual relations is not amenable to discussion, and the foundation of culture is an *a priori* notion of sexual necessity.

Once more it seems that in the substitution of conjectural history by the purity of structural abstraction the questions posed by Engels on the forms of gender differentiation implied by different conceptions of kinship have disappeared. What we can salvage from Lévi-Strauss about systems of signification may be hardly Lévi-Straussian at all.

Materialism and masculinism

If the disciples of the nineteenth-century debate on kinship appear, in rejecting the least tenable aspects of Engels' position, to have bypassed some of the crucial issues he formulated, we might expect to find in Marxist anthropology a more adequate framework through which to pose the questions we are concerned with. The centrality of the woman question to Marxism as a whole would also lead us to expect that more recent ethnography would address these issues. That this has not in fact been the case, at least within non-Soviet anthropology, has largely to do with the attention given to the potential of historical materialism as a general theory of social formations, applicable to capitalist and pre-capitalist societies alike, and on the problem of the proper relationship between Marxism and the contemporary study of pre-capitalist societies (Kahn and Llobera 1979). The problem has been whether a materialist theory of pre-capitalist formations should be derived from the commentaries by Marx on his anthropological readings, (from Morgan, Maine, and others), which could only form the basis for a viable theoretical framework by means of considerable external interpretation and extrapolation (Kahn and Llobera 1979:90); or whether the real sources for such a general theory should be deduced from the theory of capitalism itself. The disparity between the two chief protagonists, Claude Meillasoux and Maurice Godelier, over their aversion or enthusiasm for the Lévi-Straussian paradigm has also led to important differences of approach.

A third alternative has been to turn to Engels as the true founder of a *Marxist* anthropology. This position has often been rejected for the same reasons as those outlined in the introduction, namely the deviation of Engels from Marx. However, the echoes of Engels reverberate in unexpected ways in contemporary work. This is particularly true in the case of Meillasoux, and it is on his work that I shall mainly concentrate here, particularly on the approach to gender relations set out in his book *Maidens, Meal and Money (Femmes, Greniers et Capitaux)* (1975).

In many ways Meillasoux is the direct successor of Engels, whose 'foresight' was to recognize the importance of the reproduction of labour power which was largely neglected in the intervening period. Meillasoux takes this idea, which was never fully worked out by Engels, and develops it further. Like Engels, his *Maidens, Meal and Money* is an attempt to produce a theory which is historically specific, rather than universal, in the sense that theories derived from structuralism are. He particularly takes issue with Lévi-Strauss, arguing that Lévi-Strauss mistakenly sees the sexual division of labour as natural (as did Engels) and thus mistakenly believes that the 'complementarity' and 'reciprocal dependence' of male and female labour explains the institution of kinship and the universal exchange of women.

The springboard for Meillasoux's analysis is a rejection of the body of work we have considered so far in which anthropologists have prioritized kinship to the exclusion of all else. He writes, 'the notion of kinship invaded all the field, and glutted the analysis of family households, cloaking the concept of relations of production' (Meillasoux 1975:viii). In opposition to this he starts from an avowedly political stance, linking past and present in a way that is very reminiscent of *The Origin*. Like Engels, when he returns to the past, it is a past without dates or geography, and like Engels he returns to the past in order to explain the present and to speculate on the future. The object of his analysis becomes transformed in the process. The subordination of women *by* the domestic community under pre-capitalist modes of production becomes the subordination of the family as a whole by capital. The discussion of gender relations in horticultural societies is transformed into a theory of imperialism, and in this process the family comes to be seen as the last bastion against totalitarianism.

Thus, like Engels, Meillasoux gives the family a central place in a theory of history. Unlike Engels, however, it is not the innate acquisitiveness of males which is seen as the basis for women's subordination, but the 'cycle for the reproduction of human energy' (Meillasoux 1975:15). The agricultural cycle of advances and returns, the formation of permanent and indefinitely renewed social ties through time and the differential fertility of women in any given group leads to an overriding concern for any productive group with the reproduction of its membership. At an early stage of development, groups will be too small to satisfy their reproduction internally and must obtain women from other groups by capture; it is only later that this becomes regularized into an orderly process of exchange; 'power in this mode of production rests on control over the means of human reproduction – subsistence goods and wives – and not over the means of material reproduction' Meillasoux (1975:49).

We recognize both Engels and Lévi-Strauss in this suggestion. But Meillasoux's version of 'why women' does at least continue with a fleeting glance at the outcomes:

'This dependence on men as fighters does not arise because they (men) are naturally more fitted, but because they are relatively useless as reproducers. Men are more expendable and less coveted. Thus women are thrown into a situation of dependence as much in relation to men of their own group who protect them, as to men of other groups who abduct them in order to protect them in their turn. *Made inferior because of their social vulnerability*, women are put to work under male protection and are given the least rewarding, the most tedious, and above all the least gratifying tasks such as agriculture and cooking.' (Meillasoux 1975:29)

Meillasoux's personal experience in Africa, and of African migrants in metropolitan France is crucial to the overall argument of the book. It is this that enables him to conflate geographic and temporal discontinuities into a single theory. This is because he makes a direct and extraordinary association between the exploitation of migrant labour and the family under capitalism, and the pre-capitalist 'domestic economy': 'the in-between modes of exploitation and the related classes of masters and lords vanished amidst this encounter'. We may well feel that women, too, vanish in the dust clouds of the imperialist encounter. Although Meillasoux's study ought to offer a historical dimension to arguments about the significance of domestic labour, his inability to see women as more than reproducers prevents them from appearing as historical agents. Although he dissociates himself from the claim that this is a 'natural' state of affairs and acknowledges that it results from changing historical circumstances, his account has lost all the vitality of Engels' scheme. Because of their crucial role in reproduction for the agricultural 'domestic community' women are *always* controlled and this is '*always* linked to the exploitation of (their) reproductive functions'. As in many pre-class societies, kinship functions as relations of production in this mode, and control over labour through kinship is paramount. (Thus kinship is 'dominant' but not 'determinant'). Kinship is the idiom through which many forms of social interaction are organized. The 'value' of women as reproducers is historically constituted in the requirements of the domestic mode of production for labour power.

This seems to me to be a good example of Rubin's objection to the use of reproduction as an explanatory concept. What we expect the anthropological perspective to supply is an understanding of the differing ways the reproductive imperative is constructed and why some modes of production marginalize women as breeders and 'means of reproduction' in this way. Meillasoux's model of the 'domestic community' is an amalgam of a number of features of lineage-based societies, of the type of the Gouro of West Africa where his fieldwork was carried out. But conflating all agricultural modes under one evolutionary category may, as O'Laughlin suggests, 'veil considerable divergence in the organization of production, in the guise of ideological unity' (O'Laughlin 1976:21; Godelier 1980:8).

For Marxist anthropology the dominance of kinship in pre-capitalist modes has posed the problem of specifying precisely what should be regarded as 'the economy', which if defined as the forces of production seldom plays the same dominant role that it plays in capitalist societies (Kahn and Llobera 1979). Terray's interpretation of Meillasoux argues that it is not that kinship *is* economy, in this mode of production, but that the transactions, exchanges, and relationships involved in each are mutually interpenetrating (Terray 1972). However, because the status of the economy is problematic it has precedence in Meillasoux's analysis. Reproduction takes on a limited meaning as 'the conditions of existence' of the economic; it is little more than production in a cyclical sense. Women as 'the means of reproduction' are merely passive bystanders in a never-ending regeneration of granaries, tools, wives, bridewealth payments, labour, male elders, granaries, tools . . ., and so on. Because of this they are absent in other senses too. They 'never appear as vectors of the social organization. They are hidden behind men . . .' They are unable to 'create descent relations', and unable to 'acquire a status based on relations of production' (Machonochie 1983).

Once more it may be that this is an accurate reflection of the societies of which Meillasoux has direct experience, but since the 'domestic community' is a theoretical abstraction, which may or may not correspond to a number of actual societies this may not be fair comment. Meillasoux's reaction is precisely against the descriptive empiricism of bourgeois kinship studies, attempting to replace it with a materialist explanation which can reveal the underlying relations through which social forms are produced (O'Laughlin 1974). Is it then a satisfactory explanatory theory? The answer must be that it is neither a strictly materialist theory, nor a satisfactory theory of the conditions of capitalist expansion, much less of the oppression of women, since it offers no understanding of why women's valuable fertility should lead to their alienation from all rights in themselves.

The basis of sexual equality

The preceding sections have examined some of the reasons why developments in the ethnography and theory of kinship have not been used to challenge or pursue the questions raised by Engels about the determinants of sexual inequality, or to explore the relationship between the mode of production and the relations of human reproduction in the light of contemporary anthropological knowledge.

Central to Engels' formulation was the transition from matri-lineal to patrilineal society which was concomitant with the development of the forces of production, the possibility of the accumulation of surplus products, and the emergence of private property in the form of herds and slaves. Establishing the transition of kinship *forms* was crucial for Engels' subsequent argument because it enabled him to show that women lost control not only of material resources, but also of rights in their own reproductive processes. It now seems, however, that a clear-cut division between matriliny and patriliny is inaccurate. Patrilineal societies recognize matri-clans and matrilineal societies recognize patri-clans. Residential practices may also be mixed (Poewe 1981). Nor is there an easy correlation between matriliny and women's auton-omy or patriliny and their oppression. It is also unclear what criteria can usefully operate in historical and comparative state-ments of this kind. 'Power' and 'authority' have been used in a number of contradictory senses. It is also important not to confuse them with some total notion of women's position (Sacks 1979).

Furthermore, matrilineal societies do not represent a determinate position in an evolutionary sequence, but can occur in conjunction with a variety of levels of development of the productive forces (Gough 1961). True, they cluster in a fairly narrow range, but they are even to be found in the context of incipient capitalist development (Poewe 1981). The precise nexus of historical relationships posited by Engels cannot therefore be substantiated. However, his attempt to suggest a set of productive parameters that are inimical to matriliny does find general support. In particular, the contradictions between the 'distributive communalism' of matriliny and 'productive individualism' of capitalism, appear eventually to undermine the matrilineal form (Poewe 1981).

Once again nineteenth-century assumptions provide a crucial context for subsequent work. The discussion of matrilineality within anthropology was shaped by the rejection of Bachofen, Briffault and notions of matriarchal power. In replacing the wilder flights of evolutionary speculation with detailed empirical work, it was the anomaly of matrilineal societies that became most apparent. How did they deal with the organizational issues that were 'solved' through patrilineal forms? Where were they found and why were they found? Limited in number and geographical spread, what kind of adaptation did they represent? The matrilineal 'problem' became a problem from which nineteenth-century ideas could be most definitely excluded, for matriarchal power and the realities of matriliny for women were said to have little to do with each other. Although in most matrilineal societies women were at least regarded·as *jural* persons, with title to property, decision making power and control of resources (Poewe 1981:22), it was argued that adult men still had basic authority over women and children, in the person of the mother's brother, rather than the father. Often the mother's brother had 'permanent legal rights in . . . a woman's procreative powers by virtue of descent group membership' (Gough 1961:585). Thus, the conclusion was that matrilineal societies were much like patrilineal ones in terms of male rights: 'The role of women as women has been defined as that of responsibility for the care of children . . . the role of men as men is defined as having authority over women and children' (Schneider 1961:6).

Meillasoux, too, saw such societies as an earlier evolutionary form. Like many of his non-Marxist colleagues he regarded them as basically deviant, 'inflexible, unstable, and turbulent', and in a state of permanent contradiction 'which leads them either to disappear peacefully or to the risks of violent reproduction. Hence a latent tendency . . . to introduce patriliny . . . and to the adoption of a peaceful mode of circulation of women' (Meillasoux 1975:32).

Recent work has begun to re-examine these propositions more closely, and to develop an alternative analysis. Annette Weiner's study of the matrilineal Trobriands suggests that too much emphasis has been placed on descent, and that examining the control women have of the 'regenerative' aspects of human life through their control of matrilineal kin group identity reveals the extent of their power over 'transcendental' processes: birth, death, continuity, substance, ancestral essence. The power of men, their monopoly of land for example, is always conditional and can only be realized through women's control over the regenesis of the group that regards itself as 'one blood'. This 'gives women a domain of control that men can neither emulate successfully nor infiltrate with any degree of lasting power' (Weiner 1976:234). This domain is symbolically represented in women's special rituals, and materially expressed in women's wealth and cycle of exchange. Women's power comes through their control of kinship itself.

Diane Bell's examination of Kaytej women's spirituality develops the work begun by Phyllis Kaberry (1939) and Jane Goodale (1971) on Aboriginal society. Her argument, too, is that women's power over 'dreamtime' experience, the ancestral time that is thought of as a creative force linking past and present, living and dead, people and country, gives them control over a separate domain: 'it is women who keep the land alive and nurture the relationship of the living to the *jukurrpa* (dreamtime); it is through the links established by women that knowledge is transmitted and ritual reciprocity established; and it is through women's interactions with the country that the *jukurrpa* is reaffirmed and activated' (Bell 1983:230).

Both of these studies overturn long-held presuppositions about male dominance established by male fieldworkers. Both challenge assumptions about universal female subordination and replace them with positive and powerful female images. Both provide an image of women's control of crucial cultural values.

Marilyn Strathern, however, reminds us that it has been a traditional danger in anthropology to assume 'that out of particular cultures generalizations can be manufactured' (Strathern 1981). The essentialism of both accounts may be dangerous if extended beyond their cultural context. In the Trobriands, women's contribution to human reproduction is seen as a total phenomenon which embraces the regenesis of society. Should this be regarded as a universal value of 'womanness', valued by some cultures and not by others, or universally valued but usually ignored in male accounts, as Weiner appears to suggest?

I think Strathern is correct in her view that the contribution of this perspective lies in the rich new material that it presents on kinship, and gender, and in warning that it should not be used to tell us anything other than how certain cultures constitute themselves (Strathern 1981:671). Her own comparisons of the horticultural, pre-class societies of highlands New Guinea focus on the contrasts in the experience of 'womanness' between them, and the differences in 'the very manner in which symbols are generated out of gender'. Although she does not phrase it in these terms, the implications of her approach would undoubtedly be that our increasingly complex and detailed knowledge of the productive and symbolic dimensions of gender is simply not amenable at this stage to the kind of questions raised by Engels. No amount of reworking or revising will do, for we do not even know what we are comparing.

As we have seen, this view has had a well-established place in the history of anthropological thought. Nothing can be satisfactorily understood outside its own terms of reference. The abstraction of 'woman', or 'status', or 'kinship' leads merely to conceptual disaster. The challenge to androcentrism also lends itself to the detailed reconceptualization of individual societies, rather than the broad sweep of comparative assessment. While I would support this position, at least in the context of the uncritical cross-cultural studies on 'women' in the first wave of feminist anthropology, it presents a dilemma for the development of a Marxist anthropology of gender, that might address the project, if not the method of Engels.

One attempt to surmount this problem, and to provide a historical materialist reading of gender relations in four African societies is provided in the work of Karen Sacks, who takes up Engels' questions but strips them of their technologistic and evolutionary bias. Sacks underlines the tremendous variation in productive means among non-class food producers (Sacks

1979:115), which include not only means of production but different combinations of subsistence strategies. Land use, crop complex, and tools are interrelated in a variety of ways, and these are in turn related to the forces of production, the way in which people organize themselves, together with the land, tools, and seeds to perform the tasks that produce their subsistence (Sacks 1979:116). Nevertheless, she argues that underlying this diversity one can find a uniformity, which characterizes and delimits a distinct mode. It is therefore possible to identify discriminating features which have crucial implications for gender relations.

> 'Gender underlies but is not synonymous with either men's or women's relations to the means of production; each sex stands in a variety of relations to the means of production; and kinship relations – particularly those of sister and wife – are relations of production and hence relations of power' (Sacks 1979:73)

Rejecting the dualism between production and reproduction which has dogged earlier debates, and viewing kinship as political economy rather than relations of reproduction, she reinstates the Marxian unity between them that was misinterpreted by Engels. In working comparatively and historically within a limited area she identifies the power bases available to women through their own kinship-mediated relation to the productive system.

Similarly, Janet Siskind (1978) notes that kinship categories define the rights of individuals to appropriate the labour and product of the opposite sex, or across generations. She argues that an historical precondition for this is the development of increasing specialization of production. As a consequence labour is committed to activities which are productive but uncertain, or of delayed return, preventing self-sufficient subsistence on a daily basis and resulting in a sexually differentiated labour process. Thus, claims on the product of the other sex must be established, together with trans-generational rights in the procreation of future labourers. In this way relations between non-producers, producers, and future producers are ordered through the structuring of sexuality. Although Siskind does not develop this, we know that these rights can be constructed in a myriad ways. They can express temporal continuity through male or female rights, and emphasize reciprocity or asymmetry, autonomy, or alienation. Siskind's discussion suggests the possibility of an historically specific analysis of the conditions under which male rights in women become socially predominant and are legitimated, and in which spheres of female control are culturally esteemed or devalued. The symbolic and metaphorical elaboration of these relationships 'naturalizes' them as outcomes of the intrinsic qualities of men and women, and both allows and conceals contradictory representations: 'Ideology provides motive power for both men and women to share their products, embroidering necessity with mystery, relating human production to nature, spirits and sex' (Siskind 1978:868).

Both these studies, and the wide-ranging collections of papers discussed by Tsing and Yanagisako (1983), call for a revaluation of the relationship between kinship and gender. They suggest that we can now begin to reintegrate the analysis of the material basis of kinship and the construction of gender and sexual inequality, that because of history, discourse, and political allegiance have diverged during the previous hundred years.

Notes

1 This has been largely confined to the critique of the exchange of women as a defining feature of culture as propounded by Lévi-Strauss, the reanalysis of matrilineal societies, and the recent discussion of the work of Meillasoux.

References

Aaby, P. (1977) Engels and women. *Critique of Anthropology* 3(9/10):25–53.

Barnes, J.A. (1971) *Three Styles in the Study of Kinship*. London: Tavistock.

Bell, D. (1983) *Daughters of the Dreaming*. Melbourne: McPhee Gribble/ George Allen & Unwin.

Carroll, V. (1968) Nukuora kinship terms. Paper to the 67th Annual Meeting of the American Anthropological Association, Seattle, Washington.

Coward, R. (1983) *Patriarchal Precedents: Sexuality and Social Relations*. London: Routledge & Kegan Paul.

Dahlberg, F. (1981) *Woman the Gatherer*. New Haven: Yale University Press.

Eggan, F. (1972) Introduction. In P. Reining (ed.) *Kinship Studies in the Morgan Centennial Year*. Anthropological Society of Washington.

Firth, R. (1984) The sceptical anthropologist? Social anthropology and Marxist views on society. In M. Bloch (ed.) *Marxist Analyses and Social Anthropology*. London: Tavistock.

Fleming, L. (1983) Lévi-Strauss and the politics of representation. *Block* (journal of Art History Dept., Middlesex Poly.) 9:34.

Fortes, M. (1949) *The Web of Kinship Among the Tallensi*. London: Oxford University Press.

—— (1959) Primitive kinship. *Scientific American* 200 (6):146–57.

—— (1969) *Kinship and the Social Order: The Legacy of Lewis Henry Morgan*. Chicago: Aldine.

Godelier, M. (1980) The origins of male domination. *New Left Review* 127:3–17.

Goodale, J. (1971) *Tiwi Wives: a Study of Women of Melville Island, Northern Australia*. Seattle: University of Washington Press.

Gough, K. (1961) Variation in matrilineal systems: part two. In D.M. Schneider and K. Gough (eds.) *Matrilineal Kinship*. Berkeley: University of California Press.

Kaberry, P. (1939) *Aboriginal Women: Sacred and Profane*. London: Routledge & Kegan Paul.

Kahn, J. and Llobera, J. (1979) French Marxist anthropology: Twenty years after. *Journal of Peasant Studies* 8(1):81–100.

Keesing, R. (1972) Simple models of complexity: The lure of kinship. In P. Reining (ed.) *Kinship Studies in the Morgan Centennial Year*. Anthropological Society of Washington.

Korn, F. (1973) *Elementary Structures Reconsidered: Lévi-Strauss on Kinship*. London: Tavistock.

Leach, E. (1961) *Pul Eliya, A Village in Ceylon: A Study of Land Tenure and Kinship*. Cambridge: Cambridge University Press.

Leacock, E. (1972) *Myths of Male Dominance*. New York: Monthly Review Press.

Levine, N. (1972) *The Tragic Deception: Marx contra Engels*. Santa Barbara: C110 Press.

Lévi-Strauss, C. (1956) The family. In Harry L. Shapiro (ed.) *Man, Culture and Society*. New York: Galaxy/Oxford University Press.

—— (1966) *The Savage Mind*. London: Weidenfeld & Nicolson.

—— (1969) *The Elementary Structures of Kinship*. London: Eyre & Spottiswoode (English translation).

Malinowski, B. (1930) Kinship. *Man* 30:19–29.

Machonochie, M. (1983) Meillasoux's concept of the domestic community and his defence of the family. (Unpublished paper.)

Mead, M. (1935) *Sex and Temperament in Three Primitive Societies*. New York: Morrow.

Morgan, L.H. (1871) *Systems of Consanguinity and Affinity of the Human Family*. Oosterhout, NB: Anthropological Publications. (1966 edn.)

—— (1877) *Ancient Society*. Cleveland and New York: World Publishing Company. (1963 edn.)

Meillasoux, C. (1975) *Maidens, Meal and Money (Femmes, Greniers et Capitaux)*. Cambridge: Cambridge University Press.

Murdock, G. (1957) World ethnographic sample. *American Anthropologist* 59:664–87.

Needham, R. (1971) *Rethinking Kinship and Marriage*. London: Tavistock.

O'Laughlin, B. (1974) Mediation of contradiction: Why Mbum women do not eat chicken. In M. Rosaldo (ed.) *Woman, Culture and Society*. Stanford: Stanford University Press.

—— (1976) Production and reproduction. *Critique of Anthropology* 6.

Poewe, K. (1981) *Matrilineal Ideology: Male-Female Dynamics in Luapula, Zambia*. London: Academic Press.

Rubin, G. (1975) The traffic in women: Notes on the political economy of sex. In R. Reiter (ed.) *Toward an Anthropology of Women*. New York: Monthly Review Press.

—— (1984) Thinking sex: Notes for a radical theory of the politics of sexuality. In C.S. Vance (ed.) *Pleasure and Danger*. London: Routledge & Kegan Paul.

Sacks, K. (1979) *Sisters and Wives: The Past and Future of Sexual Equality*. Westport VA: Greenwood Press.

Schneider, D. (1972) What is kinship all about? In P. Reining (ed.) *Kinship Studies in the Morgan Centennial Year*. Anthropological Society of Washington.

Schneider, D. and Gough, K. (1961) *Matrilineal Kinship*. Berkeley: University of California Press.

Singer, A. (1973) Marriage payments and the exchange of people. *Man* 8:80–92.

Siskind, J. (1978) Kinship and mode of production. *American Anthropologist* 8:860–72.

Strathern, M. (1981) Culture in a netbag: The manufacture of a subdiscipline in anthropology. *Man* 16:665–88.

Tanner, N. (1982) *Becoming Human*. Cambridge: Cambridge University Press.

Terray, E. (1972) *Marxism and Primitive Societies*. New York: Monthly Review Press.

Tsing, A. and Yanagisako, S. (1983) Feminism and kinship theory. *Current Anthropology* 24(4):511–16.

Vogel, L. (1983) *Marxism and the Oppression of Women*. London: Pluto Press.

Weiner, A. (1976) *Women of Value, Men of Renown: New Perspectives on Trobriand Exchange.* Austin: University of Texas Press.

Zihlman, A. (1981) Women as shapers of the human adaptation. In F. Dahlberg (ed.) *Woman The Gatherer.* New Haven: Yale University Press.

8
Engels and the making of Chinese family policy

Delia Davin

> A thousand years from now, all of us, even Marx, Engels, and Lenin will probably appear rather ridiculous. (Mao Zedong, in Snow 1973)

Introduction

The face of Engels, along with that of Marx, is familiar to every Chinese citizen. Their portraits still hang in many public places and the features of these 'hairy grandfathers', as children call them, create an imagery of the Western male as a Victorian patriarch. Engels' full name transliterates into Chinese as *Fei-lei-di-li-ke En-ge-si*. Not surprisingly his unwieldy personal name is usually dispensed with, his surname being used on its own in all but the most formal of contexts.

Large numbers of Chinese have a basic acquaintance with the writings of Marx and Engels, and of Engels' works the best known is *The Origin of the Family, Private Property and the State*. In tertiary-level education, this work is still used as a text for political study. More importantly, as I will show, policy on women and the family has been both influenced and justified by the ideas Engels expressed in *The Origin*. The reverence still accorded to the heritage of Marx, Engels, and Lenin means that even today, when a new policy is advocated, their writings have to be sifted to provide the proponents of change with scriptural justification while its opponents use the same methods to give validity to their arguments.

China has changed enormously in recent years, not least for women. Once the function of the women displayed on advertising hoardings was to exhort people to kill flies, study, and work hard or cross the road safely. Now they grin out at the world to advertise cosmetics, washing-machines, and even Coca-Cola. During the cultural revolution, the rare Chinese with naturally curly hair sometimes had it straightened to avoid accusations of 'bourgeois affectation'; now most city women under forty have perms. Clothes were once plain, frugal, patched, but always comfortable; now fashion is asserting itself, in some cases at the expense of physical ease or comfort. Images of women have been depoliticized: for example, posters and calendars have tended in recent years to portray women as decorative rather than heroic. Consumerism is rampant; anyone who can afford it spends money on domestic furnishings and electrical goods and much energy goes into saving for and selecting these purchases.

New rural policies have transferred basic decision-making from the collective to the household level and have encouraged peasant households to invest time and resources in craft and sideline production. Most observers agree that these changes will tend to reinforce the sexual division of labour within the household and to reinforce the authority of the household head who is usually a male.

The stringent population policy which allows only a single child to each couple is supported by the slogan 'quality not quantity'. The emphasis on quality has been accompanied by a new stress on child-rearing but more particularly on mothering. Children must be brought up to be healthy, hard-working, well-educated, and moral and the mother's role in all this is usually presented as paramount.

Many of the changes which have taken place are ones which in other historical situations have been accompanied by an increased domestification of women and a reduction in their participation in the workforce. The idea that married women might be encouraged to withdraw from paid employment has in fact been raised in the

Chinese press in recent years, notably in 1980–81. As it had been admitted that urban unemployment was a serious problem, the suggestion was made that it could be solved if married women surrendered their jobs.

The National Women's Federation, China's official Party-led women's organization opposed the suggestion strongly (National Women's Federation 1983a:86–90). Its practical arguments were that the unemployed would not necessarily perform the work currently done by women, and that most families needed the wife's earnings. It relied much more heavily however on arguments of principle.[1] It sent letters to the Central Committee and to the press pointing out that the Party's policy towards women had always been based on Engels' analysis:

> 'To emancipate woman and to make her the equal of man is and remains an impossibility so long as the woman is shut out from social productive labour and restricted to private domestic labour. The emancipation of woman will only be possible when woman can take part in production on a large, social scale' (Engels 1884:221)

In all their arguments the leaders of the Women's Federation made it clear that any change of policy on women's employment, any attempt to ease married women out, would be retreating from all that the Federation, as a Party-led women's organization, had attempted to achieve in its long history.

For the moment, at least, their stand has been successful. Official policy on women still insists on the need for them to be engaged in work outside the home. At the same time, the government's struggle to reduce fertility has produced a renewed interest in women's status. Although much discussion remains at the level of ritual incantation about 'social productive labour', there is a growing realization that participation in the labour force is only a beginning and that many factors have combined to obstruct equality between the sexes. Such problems as the male-dominated kinship system, patrilocal marriage, an unofficial division of labour which often restricts women to lower-paid or subordinate jobs, and the double burden of women's responsibilities do receive some limited attention (National Women's Federation: 1983b).

Before reverting to a brief discussion on Engels' relevance in China today, I will summarize the history of the Chinese Party's policy towards women and the family to show how important the Engels heritage has been.

The C C P and the 'woman question', 1921–48

From its inception in 1921 until the counter-revolution of 1926–27, the main focus of Chinese Communist Party (CCP) activity was in Shanghai, Guangzhou, Wuhan, and the few other areas of China with a sizeable working–class population. Many of the new class of industrial workers were women, indeed in Shanghai factories they outnumbered men, so communist work among women began early. Issues such as the freedom of women to work, to choose their own husbands, to divorce, to unbind their feet, and to cut their hair were taken up by the women's departments of both the Kuomintang and the Communist Party at this time. The 'woman question' was much discussed in leftist literature and the CCP regularly passed resolutions on women's issues.

After the Kuomintang-Communist split in 1927, the communists retreated to remote rural areas, most of them in the south, where they began to set up 'soviets' or areas controlled by their armies. In 1934, under heavy military pressure, the communist armies evacuated their southern bases and set out on the Long March. Arriving in the north towards the end of 1935, they greatly expanded communist power there in what became known, during the war against Japan, as anti-Japanese base areas, or, later, liberated areas. Thus for over two decades prior to the establishment of the People's Republic in 1949, the CCP wielded state power in the areas under its military control and attempted, in very difficult conditions, to evolve social policies appropriate to a revolutionary state. Resolutions were no longer enough: the Party had to translate its aspirations for women into policies designed to change their status throughout society.

To understand communist attitudes and policies in this period, it is necessary to look a little further back in history. The Party leaders of the 1920s and 1930s had become Marxists in the great political and intellectual upsurge known as the May Fourth Movement which followed the First World War. Few Marxist classics had been translated into Chinese before this time, but Marxist ideas filtered through by way of Japanese, Western European languages, and, especially in the 1920s, Russian. The main influence of Marxist thought was on the development of the anti-imperialist movement and of a conceptual framework for the understanding of history. However, the intellectual ferment which characterized the May Fourth period produced demands for reform and modernization in many institutions, including, very importantly, the family and relationships between the sexes (Witke 1970). Within the educated élite and its fringes, there was a revolt of youth, as young people acquired individual ideals and aspirations which conflicted with traditional family *mores*. An idealized Western family model, available to Chinese through Western literature, led to an advocacy of monogamy, romantic love, free-choice marriage, and the conjugal family. Women's rights advocates, clearly under the influence of Western feminist movements, campaigned for women's right to a profession, to education, to the vote, and to own property. Over 100 papers and journals devoted to the 'woman question' – the majority quite short-lived – began publication in these years. Men seem to have been numerous among both their readers and their contributors, a reflection of the very close links, at this time, between women's emancipation and the revolt of the young of both sexes against the traditional family system.

Like other young radicals, communist leaders were affected by this current of ideas. Some of them contributed regularly to the journals devoted to the 'woman question'. Mao Zedong's first known publication was on women, forced marriage, and suicide (Witke 1967). It showed great sympathy for the tragic lives of women. Like others of his generation Mao probably supported the family revolution because of his own early experience, as well as through intellectual conviction. Much later, in 1936, he perhaps consciously echoed Engels' dictum – 'Within the family, the husband is the bourgeois, and the wife represents the proletariat'

(Engels 1884:137) – when he recalled, 'There were two Parties in the family. One was my father, the Ruling Power. The Opposition was made up of myself, my mother, and sometimes even the labourer' (Snow 1937:128).

One of the most interesting statements on the 'woman question' from this era is contained in the writing of the eclectic Marxist essayist Lu Xun, regarded as China's greatest modern writer (Lu Xun 1923). In the May Fourth period, Ibsen's *Doll's House* was an immensely popular play with the urban intelligentsia. In 1923 Lu Xun read a paper entitled 'What happens after Nora leaves home?' to students at the Peking Normal College for Women, in which he argued that Nora's real problem was her lack of economic power. Without it she would end in a brothel or would be forced to return to her husband. He reasoned that only a total reform in the economic system could give Nora and women like her economic independence, and thus save them from being dolls or puppets. Firstly, he said there would have to be a fair sharing out between men and women in the family. Secondly, men and women would have to have equal rights in society. He confessed that he did not know how all this was to be achieved but warned that it would be much harder than the attainment of political rights.

Although it is impossible to do justice to the May Fourth debate on women and the family in a few paragraphs, perhaps enough has been said to indicate its importance and the variety of its concerns. When the Communist Party began to establish soviets in the highlands of central southern China, its first attempts to reform marriage and family life were undoubtedly influenced by the radicalism of May Fourth thinking. Neither Marx nor Engels had left much guidance for their followers about what should happen to the family in the initial stages of socialism but the Chinese soviets did have the model of Soviet Russia and their 1931 marriage regulations also reflected its influence (Meijer 1971). These regulations laid down that marriage for both men and women must be based on free choice. Divorce was to be free, no grounds were necessary, and it was to be granted if both parties desired it but also at the insistence of one partner even if the other partner opposed it.

The principle that economic independence was a prerequisite for women's emancipation was reflected in the agrarian reform laws which not only transferred land from land-rich to land-poor families, but also gave women their own land. However, the preamble to the marriage regulations explained that as the suffering of women under feudal domination had been greater than that of men, and as some women still suffered from physical handicaps (such as bound feet), and had not yet acquired complete economic independence, their interests had to be protected. Consequently the man could be required to support his ex-wife and had greater financial responsibility for the children after divorce. (The same principles were observed in Soviet Russia's family codes of 1918 and 1926). In 1934 the new marriage law of the Chinese Soviet Republic incorporated a few significant changes. Although couples were still required to register a marriage, *de facto* marriages were to be registered, thus extending the protection afforded to women by legal marriage to those who had not complied with soviet law. (The Russian family code of 1926 had also extended alimony rights to women in unregistered marriages: a measure which was passed only after vigorous debate (Farnsworth 1978:143–49).)

The first limitation on total freedom of divorce was contained in an article which stipulated that the consent of a Red Army fighter was required before his wife could be granted a divorce (Meijer 1971:285).[2] Despite this caveat, the marriage legislation of the Chinese soviets, more radical than anything that was to follow, was notable for its lack of restriction on divorce. The vision on which it was based, of an easily-dissolved conjugal family formed by free choice, was quite consistent with Engels' expectation that under socialism men and women would form long-term unions founded on affection which would be dissolved if that affection cooled (Meyer 1978:95).

It was not however a vision which could easily become a reality in a society based on small-scale peasant production. Even after land reform, the basic economic unit of this society remained the family, and in the family reposed the ownership of the means of production: land, tools, and stock. The head of the family continued to organize and deploy the family labour force and both production and the reproduction of the labour force took place under his watchful eye. Marriage legislation in this period, like later communist marriage legislation, failed to confront the problem that marriage, divorce, the custody of children, and women's rights to land and other property were not just problems between individuals but had implications for the household as a productive unit.

Even in the southern soviet areas, radical policy on the family proved divisive and gave rise to problems and opposition. When the main body of the communist movement arrived in the north after the Long March, these problems intensified. The remote mountain areas of the north in which the communist bases were established were socially still more conservative than the southern countryside. Northern peasant women led more confined lives and were harder to organize. Other factors also contributed to a growing conservatism. Having been forced to abandon the south, the communist leadership, in effect fighting for survival in the north, was naturally unwilling to incur unpopularity through the pursuit of divisive radical principles. From 1937, the United Front agreement with the Kuomintang against the Japanese resulted in the moderation of a variety of policies (Selden 1972). All this was reflected in gradual changes of emphasis which became particularly noticeable in the early 1940s. Cadres working with women were urged to take the mobilization of women for production as their main task (Davin 1976:39–44). In family disputes cadres were told to work whenever possible for reconciliation. Divorce was presented only as a last resort. Divorce by mutual consent was still allowable, but if divorce was desired by only one party, grounds had to be provided and proved. The marriage laws of the different liberated areas each provided its own list of acceptable grounds such as ill-treatment, desertion, impotence, and opium addiction (Meijer 1971:285–99).

There is a tendency in recent Western writing to portray the increasingly conservative family policy of the CCP as being exclusively due to the need to retain the support of the male peasantry – if necessary by the preservation of the patriarchal family in a reformed guise (Stacey 1983; Johnson 1983). This view is certainly not without merit, but it is important to recognize that the changes were probably reassuring to a great number of women. Many middle-aged and older married women, identifying their own interests with those of their husbands' families, found radical family policies quite threatening. Furthermore, women Party leaders themselves seem to have turned increasingly against divorce on demand.

Although, among the peasants, most divorces were initiated by women, this was not so among cadres. Moreover, there were some notorious cases in which, having achieved seniority in the communist movement, male leaders divorced their old wives on the pretext that they were 'backward' in order to marry younger women (Hua 1981:106–12). Mao Zedong's own case may well have influenced opinion among women leaders. In 1937 he divorced He Zezhen who had shared his life of hardship for seven or eight years, borne him four or five children including one on the Long March, and was at the time suffering from tuberculosis. A year later, despite the disapproval of the Central Committee, he married an ex-film actress from Shanghai, Jiang Qing.[3]

From the early 1940s, as marriage policy became less radical, the other prong of work to emancipate women, their mobilization for productive labour in agriculture and the cottage textile industry, was much more strongly emphasized. This was not of course a new policy. Even in Jiangxi, the usual quotations from Engels had been used to support the argument that participation in production labour would liberate women. However, the implication then was that women should work for economic independence which alone would enable them to claim the freedom of marriage and divorce to which the law entitled them. In the northern liberated areas the argument was rather different. By performing productive labour women would strengthen their own position within the family and would increase family income, both effects which, it was agreed, would promote democracy and harmony within the family (Davin 1976).

As an explanation of women's oppression, it should be noted, a narrow emphasis on women's exclusion from production would have seemed more convincing in the north, where women's participation in agriculture was indeed low, than in the south, where they had always participated at significant levels. The new emphasis also met the real economic needs of the beleaguered liberated areas as the intensification of women's labour boosted handicraft production for the war effort and made it possible to replace men who were away fighting.

The end of the war with Japan in 1945 was followed by months of uneasy negotiations between the Kuomintang and the communists which culminated in the outbreak of civil war in 1946. Agrarian policy underwent an abrupt change with the reintroduction of a land reform programme, a policy which had been shelved at the beginning of the United Front. Perhaps partly because they were encouraged to take an active role in land reform and were once more able to gain their own share of land, there seems to have been a surge of militancy among women at the grass roots in this period. Despite the cautions that 'contradictions between men and women should not be treated as antagonistic', men who were known to beat their wives were sometimes themselves seized and beaten by angry female militants (Belden 1949:275–308).

The People's Republic: Marriage law and collectivization

After the establishment of the People's Republic of China in 1949, land reform and marriage reforms were carried out across the whole country. The marriage law of 1950 was one of the new state's first laws. Efforts to implement its provisions culminated in a big campaign in 1953. Unfortunately the consequences for women sometimes proved disastrous. There was a tremendous backlash of violence against young women who refused arranged marriages or who attempted to obtain a divorce. Village cadres were unable, and sometimes unwilling, to provide sufficient protection. The situation of the wife who claimed both a divorce and land rights was especially hazardous. Her enraged husband would see himself as losing both a wife for whom he had paid, and part of the family land. Tens of thousands of women are known to have been murdered (Davin 1976:87). Many other cases were presumably hushed up. Part of a woman's vulnerability was that, as an outsider in her husband's village, she had little hope of sympathy or help either from her neighbours or from the village cadres who had grown up with him and might indeed be his kin. Shaken by this violent reaction, the government brought the 1953 campaign to a close. Though the law remained in force, subsequent attempts to implement it proceeded far more cautiously.

Collectivization in China was carried through by degrees in the 1950s. Full collective farming was established under the commune system of the late 1950s which, with some adjustments, was then maintained for two decades. Women were promised great advantages from collectivization and the abolition of the family as a socioeconomic unit. To quote from one such authoritative statement:

'Today, following the disappearance of private ownership and of the small producer economy, the family is no longer a socioeconomic unit. Ended too is the patriarchal family relation under which, for thousands of years, the man oppressed the woman and the woman relied on the man for her means of life, in which the patriarch oppressed all other members of the family and they relied on him for their living.'   (Fan 1960:56)

Engels was often quoted to show that the end of private ownership of land and the means of production would finally make possible an effective reform of the marriage system:

'Full freedom of marriage can therefore only be generally established when the abolition of capitalist production and of the property relations created by it has removed all the accompanying economic considerations which still exert such a powerful influence on the choice of marriage partner. For then there is no other motive left except mutual affection.'   (Engels 1884:144)

However, the authorities were sensitive to the accusation that collectivization amounted to the abolition of the family, so sensitive indeed that, whereas Engels had been vague about the future of the family, they were prepared to be definite:

'The breaking down of the system of patriarchy will not and cannot lead to the "destruction" or "elimination" of the family.

. . . The family, as a form of joint life of two sexes united in
marriage we may definitely say, will never be eliminated. The
existence of this form of joint life is dictated not only by the
physiological difference of sexes but also by the perpetuation of
the race. Even in the communist society we cannot conceive of
any objective basis and necessity for the "elimination of the
family".'   (Fan 1960:58)

Alas, time was to show that collectivization did not transform the
peasant family to the extent which had been envisaged. The
position of women did show improvements. Polygamy, concubin-
age, child betrothal, and the worst forms of forced marriage were
eliminated. Women succeeded in exercising their rights to jobs,
education, property, divorce, and custody of children with
increasing frequency. But despite all these improvements women
are still clearly disadvantaged in many areas of life. Sons who stay
with the family are still preferred to daughters who marry out. In
the countryside where marriage continues to have major economic
repercussions for the whole household, a modified form of
arranged marriage and brideprice are still common. Women are
still grossly under-represented in political and managerial posts.

   The factors involved in women's continuing subordination are of
course complex, but Engels' insight into the connection between
the small-producer economy and patriarchal power remains
relevant. Even after collectivization, important elements of the
domestic economy survived. Private plot production and household sidelines, both outside the collective economy, continued to
supply an important proportion of household needs. Housing was
usually privately owned and under the *de facto* control of the
household head, normally the oldest working male. The state not
only failed to challenge the concept of the household head, it
underwrote his authority. For example, income from the collective
was usually paid directly to him rather than to the individual who
had earned it. The household head represented his family at
important meetings, made the census declarations, and might even,
as in imperial China, be held responsible for the behaviour of the
members of his family. Given the continuation of the family as an

income-pooling unit, it was only natural that the head continued to claim an interest in the marriages of its members. Marriage itself was costly and had to be saved for. Furthermore, through marriage, families gained or lost labour power and ensured the long-term reproduction of labour.

The rural reforms: Implications for the family

Although women remained subordinate within the family, it seems certain that collectivization did improve their situation. It is hard to see how this improvement can be maintained under the present system (Davin 1984). Since 1979, collective production has increasingly given way to family farming. Land is now contracted out to individual households. Within certain limitations, they take their own production decisions and, after the delivery of quotas to the state, retain what they have produced for sale or consumption. Domestic crafts and other non-agricultural family enterprises have grown very rapidly. The result is that rural China is now clearly once more a small-producer economy of which the family is the basic socioeconomic unit. This 'family' is again discussed as an undifferentiated unit. For example the devolution of management and decision-making to the household is hailed as a democratic process, although in practice it usually means that the household head resumes direct control over the labour of its other members and over the means of production. Women continue to perform much of the agricultural labour but they are especially prominent in the flourishing family sidelines, many of which are extensions of traditional women's work. In an analysis which again uses the link made by Engels between women's exclusion from productive labour and their subjection, it is claimed that these enterprises, by allowing women to contribute more to family income, are promoting their equality. The connection which Engels also made between private property, family forms, and the subjection of women, which under collectivization was considered important, is once more being ignored (Wu 1983).

While it is doubtless true that women may gain in status from their participation in such enterprises, and that they will benefit from the growing prosperity of the countryside, the reforms have left them more than ever dependent on their relationships with men. The household contracts for land through the household head and the equipment for household enterprises is privately owned. A divorcee or a woman who remarried after the death of her husband would thus lose the access to land or the means of production which she had enjoyed through her relationship to her husband. It is unlikely that she would be allowed to take much with her.

Although under Chinese law, property acquired during marriage is the joint property of the spouses, and husband and wife have the right to inherit from each other (Marriage Laws 1950, 1981), women's property rights have been difficult to implement in rural society. At the time of writing (April 1985), the National People's Congress is divided on whether a spouse should be entitled to inherit all the property of the deceased partner, or only one half of it with the other half going to the parents and children of the deceased (*Guardian* 1985). This debate, like earlier attempts to deal with property and inheritance, is problematic because the law attempts to deal in terms of individual rights, but in peasant society much property is still seen as belonging to the family as a unit. Women, whose membership of the family is dependent on their relationship to a man, are thus vulnerable. With the growth of private enterprise in both the agricultural and the non-agricultural economy the loss to women where their property rights are poorly enforced is now considerable.

The single-child family policy

Today Engels is being quoted to legitimize a wholly new policy. Faced with a severe shortage of arable land, a very young population, and the possibility of a demographic explosion, the Chinese authorities have introduced a draconian policy under which couples are not allowed to have more than one child (Croll, Davin, and Kane 1985).

When Mao and his followers still thought that a large population was an economic asset, they insisted that Marxism showed the answer to high population growth was not birth control but

increased production. The advocates of birth control were condemned as 'Malthusianists' (Walker 1964). This line was finally
abandoned in 1962 and the family-planning campaign was revived,
intensifying over the years until it culminated in 1979 in the
single-child policy. As part of the campaign, arguments were
produced to show that birth control measures were not of
themselves Malthusian.

> 'First Marxism is never opposed to the adoption by mankind of
> necessary measures in the control of reproduction. Engels said on
> this question "at any rate, it is for the people in communist
> society themselves to decide when and how this is to be done,
> and what means they wish to employ for the purpose".' (Liu
> 1981)

The Engels quotation is taken from a letter to Karl Kautsky in
which Engels, while refuting the idea that over-population was a
real problem in their own time, admitted the possibility that it
might one day become one. When the introduction of the one-child
family policy in 1979 created a need to justify state intervention in
reproduction, the same letter was used: 'But if at some stage
communist society finds itself obliged to regulate the production of
human beings, just as it has already come to regulate the
production of things, it will be precisely this society and this
society alone, which can carry this out without difficulty.' (Engels
1881)

Birth-control propaganda has even taken up Engels' neglected
assertion that:

> 'the determining factor in history is the production and
> reproduction of immediate life. This, again, is of a twofold
> character: on the one side, the production of the means of
> existence, of food, clothing, and shelter, and the tools necessary
> for that production; on the other side, the production of human
> beings themselves, the propagation of the species.' (Engels
> 1884:71)

This two-fold definition of production is used to justify the
demand that people should respond to state-imposed targets for

both production and reproduction. The demand itself is underwritten by a system of rewards and penalties under which couples who comply with their reproduction quotas are rewarded and those who do not are penalized (Croll, Davin, and Kane 1985). But the one-child family policy is relevant to this paper not just because its promoters seek to legitimize it with quotations from Engels. With this policy, as with policies on marriage and divorce and the attempt to redefine the roles of women, the state is heading for a clash with the interests of the patriarchal peasant family. As we have seen, in earlier confrontations compromises were sought. In this one, the state seems less prepared to compromise. It is therefore forced to confront the widespread existence of son preference among the peasants, the fact that peasant families are unwilling at all times to content themselves with a single child, but are especially unlikely to do so, no matter what the pressure may be, if that child is female. The re-emergence of female infanticide illustrates in the most tragic and dramatic way possible just how profound this preference is. It amounts to the fact that some families whose first-born is female are prepared to kill the child if that is the only way to be allowed another try for a boy. In the past, instances of discrimination against women tended to be explained as 'the remnants of feudal thought', the implication being that they had no material basis in today's society. Now, although this explanation is still often trotted out, a better analysis is also being sought. Official publications recognize that universal patrilocal marriage, and the consequent need for sons because they alone can allow the family to reproduce its labour force, inevitably gives rise to son preference. As yet, no real solution to the problem has been found, but at least it is being more directly faced and discussed than in the past. Moreover the Women's Federation has been able to use the evidence of the discrimination against girls revealed by the single-child campaign to promote campaigns for women's rights and, as we saw at the beginning of this paper, to oppose conservative initiatives on women.

Conclusion

As we have seen, Engels' writing on women and the family was, and is still, influential in China. For over sixty years, his major work, *The Origin of the Family, Private Property and the State* has been the basis for the formulation of policy on women and the family. Hardly surprisingly, Engels' analysis of women's oppression, written in capitalist nineteenth-century Europe, did not entirely fit the circumstances of an Asian peasant society developing along a different political and economic path. A mechanistic use of Engels' analysis tended to blind the communist movement to some important factors in the oppression of Chinese women. It must be assumed that his prescriptions for women's emancipation – even had it been possible to carry them through fully – might have been found wanting in some respects. Nevertheless, their partial implementation has certainly produced some improvements for women.

The post–Mao government, despite its claims to pragmatism and flexibility, still finds it useful to explain its policies by recourse to quotations from Marxist classics. This habit of course predates Marxism in China: Confucian texts were once used in the same way. Chinese policy-makers today are perhaps the more attracted by this time-honoured form of legitimization because in many areas of economic policy they are making real departures from Marxist orthodoxy.

These departures have already had some adverse effects on women, as for example in the strengthening of the rural family as a socioeconomic unit. In urban employment, on the other hand, as we have seen, women's interest groups were able to defend the gains already made by women through an appeal to orthodoxy. If future policy is indeed to be governed by economic pragmatism, it may no longer be possible to defend women's interests in the same way. The need for a strong women's movement will arise but it is not clear how that could be satisfied. Meanwhile, however, whatever the limitations of Engels' legacy, it at least helped to put women's emancipation on the agenda of one of the most far-reaching revolutions in history.

Notes

1 In this account of the debate I am relying both on my general reading of
   the Chinese press, and on information given to me by officials of the
   Women's Federation on a visit to Beijing in March 1981.
2 From 1941, communist legislation retained this clause but substituted
   the word spouse for wife so that it could be used to protect soldiers of
   either sex (Fukushima and Miyasaka 1970:68).
3 Very little of Mao's personal history was known to the Chinese public
   before the Cultural Revolution and even then many details were left
   vague. Western sources differ slightly on dates of marriages and on the
   numbers of his children. I have here followed Hua Chang-ming (1981)
   whose sensible study seems to resolve most of the confusion.

References

Belden, J. (1949) *China Shakes the World*. New York: Harper.
Croll, E. (ed.) (1974) *The Women's Movement in China*. London: Anglo-
   Chinese Educational Institute.
—— (1981) *The Politics of Marriage in Contemporary China*. Cambridge:
   Cambridge University Press.
Croll, E., Davin, D., and Kane, P. (eds.) (1985) *China's One-Child Family
   Policy*. London: Macmillan.
Davin, D. (1976) *Woman-work: Women and the Party in Revolutionary China*.
   Oxford: Clarendon Press.
—— (1984) The effects of post-Mao rural reforms on the employment and
   status of Chinese peasant women. Paper presented to the Annual
   Conference of The British Sociological Association, Bradford Uni-
   versity.
Engels, F. (1881) Letter of 1 February to Karl Kautsky. In R.L. Meek
   (1953) *Marx and Engels on Malthus*. London: Lawrence & Wishart, pp.
   108–10.
—— (1884) *The Origin of the Family, Private Property and the State*. New
   York: International Publishers. (1972 edn.)
Fan, Royu (1960) Why we have abolished the feudal patriarchal system.
   Red Flag 5. Translated in E. Croll (1974) *The Women's Movement in
   China*. London: Anglo-Chinese Educational Institute.
Guardian (1985) Inheritance divides China's legislators. 9 April.
Farnsworth, B.B. (1978) Bolshevik alternatives and the Soviet family. In
   D. Atkinson, A. Dalin, and G.W. Lapidus (eds) *Women in Russia*.
   Brighton: Harvester.
Fukushima, M. and Miyasaka, H. (eds) (1970) *Marriage Laws of the Chinese
   Soviet Republic and the Chinese Liberated Areas*. Tokyo: China Research

Society. (In Japanese.)

Hua Chang-ming (1981) *La Condition Feminine et Les Communistes Chinois en Action*. Paris: Centre de Recherches et de Documentation sur la Chine Contemporaine.

Johnson, K.A. (1983) *Women, the Family and Peasant Revolution in China*. Chicago: Chicago University Press.

Liu Zheng (ed.) (1981 *China's Population: Problems and Prospects*. Beijing: New World Press.

Lu Xun (1923) What happens after Nora leaves home? In Lu Xun (1980) *Selected Works*. Translated by Gladys Yang and Yang Xian-yi. Beijing: Foreign Languages Press.

Marriage Law (1950) *The Marriage Law of the People's Republic of China*. Beijing: Foreign Languages Press.

—— (1981) *The Marriage Law of the People's Republic of China*. Beijing: Foreign Languages Press.

Meijer, M.J. (1971) *Marriage Law and Policy in the Chinese People's Republic*. Hong Kong: Hong Kong University Press.

Meyer, A.G. (1978) Marxism and the women's movement. In D. Atkinson, A. Dalin, and G.W. Lapidus (eds) *Women in Russia*. Brighton: Harvester.

National Women's Federation (1983a) Letter of 15 August from the Secretariat to comrades Wan Li and Peng Chong. In National Women's Federation (ed.) *Selected Women's Movement Documents from the Period of the Four Great Modernizations (1981–83)* (in Chinese). Beijing: Chinese Women's Press.

—— (1983b) Report of the Fifth National Congress. Beijing domestic broadcast monitored in Survey of World Broadcasts, 12 October.

Selden, M. (1972) *The Yenan Way*. Boston: Harvard University Press.

Snow, E. (1937) *Red Star Over China*. London: Gollancz.

—— (1973) *The Long Revolution*. New York: Vintage Books.

Stacey, J. (1983) *Patriarchy and Socialist Revolution in China*. Berkeley: University of California Press.

Witke, R. (1967) Mao Tse-tung, women and suicide. In M. Young (ed.) (1973) *Women in China: Studies in Social Change and Feminism*. Ann Arbor: Center for Chinese Studies, University of Michigan.

—— (1970) *Transformation of Attitudes towards Women during the May Fourth Era of Modern China*. Unpublished PhD Thesis, University of California, Berkeley.

Walker, K. (1964) Ma Yin-chu: A Chinese discussion on planning for balanced growth. In C.D. Cowan (ed.) (1964) *The Economic Growth of China and Japan*. London: Allen and Unwin.

Wu, Naitao (1983) Rural women and new economic policies. *Beijing Review* 7 March.

Name index

Aaby, P. 99, 118
Acton, W. 24
Alexander, S. 26, 31, 69, 87
Althusser, L. 4
Anderson, M. 25, 27

Baader, O. 2
Bachofen 100
Barnes, J.A. 126, 130
Barrett, M. 16, 62, 95–6
Bebel, A. 1
Beechey, V. 4, 16, 87
Belden, J. 154
Bell, D. 138
Beneria, L. 24
Bentham, J. 47
Blake, J. 47
Brenner, J. 17, 24, 26, 62
Breuer, J. 72–3

Carpenter, E. 92
Carroll, V. 121
Chodorow, N. 22, 66–8
Clark, A. 23, 24, 26, 27
Collins, R. 47
Cottrell, P.L. 21
Coward, R. 114, 118, 127, 130
Croll, E. 158, 160

Dahlberg, F. 114
Davies, M.L. 62
Davin, D. 8; on Chinese family policy 145–63
de Beauvoir, S. 3, 4, 59
Delphy, C. 16
Dinnerstein, D. 64–6
Draper, H. 3

Edholm, F. 16
Eggan, F. 116
Ehrenreich, B. 88
Eisenstein, Z.R. 16
Ellis, H. 92
Engels, F. see Subject index
Evans, M. 6; on materialism and monarchy 81–97; on socialism and feminism 1–10

Falwell, J. 71
Fan, Royu 155–56
Farnsworth, B.B. 151
Farr, W. 29
Ferguson, A. 16
Feuerbach, L.A. 57
Finch, J. 91
Firestone, S. 16
Firth, R. 113–14
Fleming, L. 127–28
Folbre, N. 16
Fortes, M. 116, 121, 126
Foster, J. 21, 22
Foster, R. 23
Fourier, C. 3
Freud, S. 6, 58, 69, 72–8, 118

Subject index